GROW TO
LIVE

A simple guide to
growing your own
good, clean food

GROW TO LIVE

A simple guide to growing your own good, clean food

Pat Featherstone

JACANA

First published by Jacana Media
(Pty) Ltd in 2009

10 Orange Street
Sunnyside
Auckland Park 2092
South Africa
(+27 11) 628-3200
www.jacana.co.za

ISBN 978-1-77009-650-9

Set in Caslon 10/15pt

Printed and bound in Malaysia for Imago

Job no. 000760

See a complete list of Jacana titles
at www.jacana.co.za

Contents

Foreword

The most important freedom is freedom from want. Food comes first. As nations, communities or individuals, there can be no real independence unless we can feed ourselves and all our people. There can be no lasting peace or security for anyone while hunger and poverty (and in their wake disease, frustration and degradation) stalk our land.

Relying on other people to produce our most basic needs leaves us terribly vulnerable. Food production on a vast scale by fewer and still fewer individuals on large profit-orientated agro-business combines is very dangerous, socially and often environmentally.

Big is definitely not beautiful. Rising production expenses due to dependence on petro-chemical industries for fuel, fertilisers and pesticides create spiralling costs and further inflation.

We have an enormous potential of untrained human beings in this country who all have to eat, need to work and have a right to a decent, satisfying life. They cannot all be trained and absorbed, even in the very long term, by commerce and industry. These, in any case, are busily engaged in the production of an ever-increasing and sometimes ridiculous range of non-essential consumer goods. These activities sometimes produce most undesirable side-effects on the environment and humanity.

Our values have become distorted; we have no time; our lives are too complicated; we need a simpler, more wholesome mode of existence that is more in harmony with Nature. This tremendous, dormant people-power needs channelling into more basic, satisfying self-help activities, of which sound survival agriculture, paying due respect to our natural resources, must come first. We do not need more expensive (problem-creating) machinery to take away work from many hands. We need to give ordinary humble folk back their self-respect as providers of food and shelter for their families.

People who have become dispossessed of their land, or have left it drawn by the big city lights, are at great risk. There is much evil, frustration and disillusionment in crowded urban slums. Smaller, more manageable centres in depopulated rural areas with enough amenities to provide a fulfilling life would seem to be the answer. In his famous book *Small is Beautiful*, by the late EF Schumacher, he deals brilliantly with this theme. Things are more personal, people care; life is less harsh in smaller communities.

Inexpensive appropriate technology can assist rural people to a better life. There are many people and organisations doing valuable pioneering work in this field.

With our variable and often difficult climate – violent winds, periodic droughts, heat waves, flash floods and the like – we need to nurture and cherish our topsoil. We can afford no advancing deserts, no dustbowls. A man with a small piece of land which he owns and on which he relies for his food must learn to love that land and care for it wisely. He must respect God's mighty Creation. Health and happiness are the direct result of living in harmony with God's natural laws.

I am grateful that my many years of voluntary work are being carried on enthusiastically, creatively and so successfully by Pat and the *Soil for Life* team. May their efforts be blessed, and may this book see a great spurt in the number of people who grow 'little patches of salvation'.

'While the earth lasts, seedtime and harvest......
shall never cease.' (Genesis 8: 22)

THE LATE MARIE ROUX, ALIAS NOKWENZA
FORMERLY OF *OPERATION GROW*
PETERVALE FARM, CERES, WESTERN CAPE
(MARIE PASSED AWAY ON 22 APRIL 2009.)

Acknowledgements

To all the incredible women (and men) who have shared my journey through life and have been an integral part of my learning:

My three precious daughters who have cheered from the sidelines all these years and have such faith in me as a mother, albeit an eccentric one. It is to them that I dedicate this book in the hope that they will tread the same path and learn the most important skill of all – to grow their own food. It is for them that I have pursued the work that I do. I want them to have the same beautiful, unspoilt world that I remember as a child. It is only by collective action that this dream will come true for them and their children.

My mother, Joan Featherstone, whose passion for gardening and animals shaped my life in more ways than one. She taught me the value of a good heap of cow manure and was never embarrassed to collect dry grass and leaves from the roadside to mulch her flower and veggie beds. At the ripe age of 85, she is still growing veggies, but this time round in pots.

My three sisters, Wuzz, Pud and Nan, who are my most cherished friends. The fact that they are such shining stars is what has driven me to search for my own light.

My aunt, Betty Hanratty, who, many years ago, introduced me to Food Gardens Foundation in Johannesburg. My eyes were opened to a whole new world and I embarked on an adventure that will never end. Betty is my mentor and friend and a source of remarkable ideas and information.

The late Marie Roux (alias Nokwenza) whose dedication to feeding people the healthiest food, and teaching poor communities to grow it, has inspired me for years. Special thanks to her for the title of this book and for her unwavering faith in my ability to carry on the message of 'growing to live'.

Joy Niland of Food Gardens Foundation, for the wealth of knowledge she passed on while I worked with her, and her very gentle way of putting it across to all those people who crossed her path over many, many years. What an incredibly inspiring person she is.

The late Polly Anderson for the sparky ideas we triggered together and the energy that flowed between us as words poured out onto paper. Our work together will continue. I feel her nudge on my shoulder when I write things wrong.

My family and friends who have taken part in the photographic shoots, and lent their hands and feet to give the book a more familial touch.

All my special friends who have held my hand through thick and thin. Without their encouragement I wouldn't have left the starting blocks.

Justin Patterson of Chef-on-Call for his great ideas for compotes, sorbets, jams, juices and jellies made out of weird and wonderful things. He's a most wonderful cook.

Leah Hawker, my middle daughter, who maintains she's a clone of her mother. Ag, shame! What a pleasure it has been working with her, as photographer and illustrator. She has the remarkable knack of knowing exactly what I want, and presenting it better than I ever thought possible. I am truly blessed to be able to work with her and look forward to many years ahead of joint projects.

Mike Kantey who phoned me out of the blue and triggered the book. What synchronicity!

Janet Bartlet, Bridget Impey and their team at Jacana who have worked so patiently alongside Leah and me while we came to terms with putting a book together. We never realised how much work it was going to be. What an ordeal for them. I take my hat off to them all.

Pat Featherstone (standing) was born, raised and educated in Zimbabwe. She is a teacher by profession, director of a non-profit organisation, *Soil for Life*, a passionate lover of Nature, the proud mother of three beautiful daughters, an about-to-be grandmother, and friend to a host of animals, furred and feathered. It is her deep concern for the future of the planet that has prompted her to use her teaching skills to help people to help themselves to a better life and, in so doing, to live in harmony with Nature.

Leah Hawker is a freelance photographer, based in Cape Town, focusing on botany, fashion and beauty. Her fine-art body of work deals with gender issues and stereotyping through the photographic process, as well as mixed media. Total animal and nature lover herself, Leah enjoyed being part of the process of creating *Grow to Live* with her mother Pat Featherstone. Lively participation from friends and family (human and animal alike) made for a wholesome, hearty and entertaining experience. Their involvement added ambience to the documentation process.

Introduction

Knowledge is like a ball.
The more you know
The bigger the surface of the unknown.

For some time now, we have been experiencing a knowledge explosion, which makes it difficult to keep up with all that we need to learn and understand. As an aspiring food gardener, you might easily be confused, to say the least, especially when our prize vegetable garden is under attack from some undercover agent.

We're all on this fragile planet together. Our future depends on our ability to help each other towards a better quality of life. And, most often, it is simply about knowing what to do. This means reading as much as we can, and communicating with other people who often have insights and understandings that are different to ours. They are looking at life with a different set of eyes. Our shared experiences and knowledge are so much richer and more meaningful, more wide-ranging and effective when dealing with attacks on one's very essence: the veggie patch.

That is what this book is all about. It's about giving people a foundation of knowledge, understanding and skills on which to build their own research and practices, and the courage to get on with it, come what may. It's simple, it's fun and immensely rewarding to grow your own food, or as much as space and time will allow. Not only this, but there are enormous benefits to your health and that of your family in partaking of fresh, safe food that you have grown in rich, natural soil, using your own household and garden waste and your own hands.

Never underestimate the needs of the other aspects of your being either: the need for peace and quiet and solitude; for fresh air and sunshine; for the connection with the Divine that comes with being in, and with, Nature; and for pure relaxation. There's also the need for exercise in the midst of our fiercely urban lives that seem to have gone astray.

Consider these things when you embrace this new passion. These are the spin-offs on which you cannot place a monetary value, but you know that your life has been turned around once you've dug that first shovelful of earth.

On a different level, you'll find that people with their hands in the soil are the ones you will seek out in the future. New and lasting friendships are forged around the veggie patches of the world. Exchanging ideas, new pieces of information, discussing successes and challenges, bartering seeds, seedlings and even your harvests, link people of all ages, colours and creeds. Food gardening has a way of overcoming all barriers.

Then, of course, there is the awesome responsibility of each and every individual on the planet not only to take responsibility for their own futures, but to take care of Mother Earth. If every home- and landowner were to act in an ethical and responsible fashion towards their piece of the Earth and to fiercely protect the life thereon, imagine how different the world would be. As my mother always used to tell me, "charity starts at home" and "a journey of a thousand miles starts with a single step".

If, in any way, we're to sort out the mess that human-kind has made of this magnificent earth, then surely each contribution, even if it is to follow the steps in this book, will have an impact. Become the custodian of your own piece of the planet; grow your own food using the principles taught to us by Nature and, if it's not your daily repast you want to grow, the same principles apply to the rest of the green plant kingdom and the tilling of the soil.

Nature does not hurry,
but everything is accomplished.

The information contained in these pages has been gleaned over many years from newspapers, magazines, books, courses, conversations with wonderful, knowledge-able people, radio and television programmes, hundreds of questions asked, and through trials and tribulations. It has all been put into practice through the years, and many gardens have flourished in southern Africa using these very simple, low-cost, water-conserving, rubbish-devouring, environment-friendly, people- and community-building techniques. The buzz word to encompass this holistic approach would be "organic". This has come to mean a lot of things to a lot of people; more about that in Chapter 1. The book has been written about growing food plants with southern Africa in mind, and the many challenges that we face in the future, not the least of which are the alarming reports that reach us almost every day.

Take the AIDS pandemic, for example. With so many afflicted people not having access to food, let alone the sort of food that will boost depressed immune systems, there is genuine cause for concern. To compound the problem, medication cannot be taken on empty stomachs.

Encouraging patients and their families to secure their own source of daily vegetables is providing them with a survival mechanism second to none. Easily available, low-cost food, grown right outside the back door, solves many immediate problems for many, and also means that travel money does not have to be found for trips to shops and supermarkets, which often adds enormously to the actual cost of what is consumed.

We do not know what future growing conditions will be like, but it appears from all reports that we are going to be hard hit. Of four major plant requirements for healthy growth and development – nutrients, air, water and an optimal growing temperature – there are two that are at severe risk. Rising global temperatures accompanied, in the Southern Hemisphere, by more frequent and severe droughts, are going to impact on food production in a very serious way. Fruit, vegetables, nuts and seeds will never again be as abundant, and as cheap, as at present. And all this with the world population continuing its exponential growth.

There is a sense of urgency here. Our food supply is vulnerable. Large-scale production on commercial farms will become increasingly difficult and costly. People are going to have to search for alternative ways of doing things. Home food gardens have to be the option. If every person grew something – whether it be on a kitchen windowsill; in a bath tub outside the back door; in the gardens of homes, schools, clinics, churchyards, police stations; using water harvested off roofs, with every bit of organic waste returned to the soil via the compost heap and earthworms – then there would be plenty of hope for the future.

Join the food gardening network today.

Tomorrow is already too late.

CHAPTER ONE

Why organic?

You probably have this book in your hands because you have already found out the truth behind the food that you're eating every day. Equally probable is that you've been bringing your family up on that food. Maybe you're thinking to yourself that, after all you've read and heard, today's food is *not* actually fit to eat – not by humans, nor by any form of life. You have made a conscious decision to take your own health, and the health of those closest to you, into your own hands.

Whether this is true or not, let's look at a few alarming details about our daily fare. If you haven't yet pondered the question "Why organic?" then perhaps you will, once you have more information at your fingertips.

We are becoming more aware of a range of "organic" products on supermarket shelves and at farmers' markets and many of us are buying them. But what lies behind the term? What does it actually mean in everyday lingo? The story goes back some years to people like Alexis Carrel, Rudolf Steiner, J I Rodale and Sir Albert Howard – all of whom recognised the truths about what was happening with food production.

What is "organic" gardening?

Sir Albert Howard first used the term "organic" in the 1920s. He told his fellow horticulturists that their approach to farming and gardening should include the sense of "wholeness, unity, integration and a natural balance". Yet, it was only after the 1960s – when the growing environmental movement made people aware of the increasing pollution levels of soil and water, and of the potential impact on their health – that the word became a part of everyday conversation.

You may have heard other words being used, such as "ecological", "biological", "alternative", "natural", "green" or "nature-friendly", but these days when people use the word "organic" they usually refer to farming or gardening methods that:

- make the best use of the "goods and services" that nature provides and that do not damage the environment;
- build and maintain the fertility of the soil by constantly adding organic matter (dead plant and animal remains) in the form of compost, humus, manure and mulch instead of using artificial fertilisers;
- do not make use of man-made pesticides, herbicides, fungicides and the like; and
- minimise all forms of pollution.

In fact, using organic methods of gardening and farming helps to restore and to heal the Earth and all of its inhabitants. By using what nature provides, we are using renewable resources, such as manure compost, leaf mould, insect predators, nutrient cycles, and so on. Just think about what nature offers us in its directory of goods and services. You'll be surprised at how much comes for free.

As you will read later on in this book, we discuss other important reasons for growing your own food: water conservation; reducing the cost of food; recycling and the reduction of solid waste. With a little bit of thought, you will be able to add a few of your own ideas. Perhaps you might simply want to be kinder to your fellow humans and garden creatures.

Firstly, the soil is the source of the nutrients that we need to sustain human health:

- **calcium** for teeth and bones, for the contraction of muscles, effective nerve functioning and for assisting with the clotting process of blood;
- **iron** for healthy blood;
- **sodium** for nerve and muscle function;
- **zinc** for the healing of wounds and the activity of many metabolic enzymes; and so you go on.

Yet, agricultural practices are robbing the soil, leaving it depleted of these essential elements, and destroying both the life in it and its inherent structure.

Around the world, and particularly since the advent of the Green Revolution (more about that later), precious topsoil is being lost at alarming rates. Depleted nutrient levels in declining amounts of topsoil contribute to the declining health of the Earth's inhabitants.

Ever wondered why more and more nutritionists are advising their lack-lustre patients to take supplements? The food you eat simply doesn't have what it should. And don't think that by pouring artificial fertilisers onto your soil you will circumvent the problem. Research has shown that food grown with synthetic (man-made) fertilisers is not as nourishing as food grown as Nature intended it to be grown. For a start, the artificial fertilisers dissolve readily in soil water, are taken up indiscriminately by the plants, and stimulate growth at an unprecedented rate, also increasing water uptake. The results of all of this?

- Watery fruit and vegetables that do not have the delicious flavour of those that have been allowed to grow at their own pace, as Nature dictates. They lack the life forces which are drawn from the Cosmos and from rich, fertile soil teeming with microbes and other forms of life and which contribute to the healthy growth of the plants.

- Lower nutrient levels in the crops.
- Plants with a reduced capacity to fight attacks by pests and diseases, and hence the necessity for the farmer or gardener to bring out the chemical ammunition, which leaves a toxic residue undetectable by the unsuspecting consumer.
- Depleted soil for the next crop.

The second truth? It doesn't make sense to spray poison all over your food before you eat it. That's exactly what is happening out there, and either consumers are not aware of this fact or they are putting their heads in the sand like the proverbial ostrich. Ask yourself how keen you would be to take home a cabbage from the most elite supermarket, if it showed signs of having been nibbled by a caterpillar? Yet, perfect produce comes with a price tag that hits your wallet, your health, and that of the planet.

Perfect produce: a point to ponder
"Extreme importance is attached by
[people in the Northern Hemisphere
and others] to the appearance of
[imported] food. Some 20% of all
agrochemicals (fertilisers and pesticides)
used serve only to improve the look
of vegetables and fruit."
(MYERS, 1985)

More on the poisonous aspects of the food you've been eating

There's a whole lot of quite shocking information about this, only a fraction of which is presented here. Look at it. Think about it. Educate yourself by reading more of the hidden dangers lurking at every mouthful.

Dr Vyvyan Howard of Liverpool University reports that

… we have in our bodies what is estimated to be at least 300 to 500 potentially harmful chemicals. Most could not have been there fifty years previously simply because they did not exist.

Dr Vyvyan Howard

Many of these synthetic chemicals are the pesticides and herbicides that are sprayed onto agricultural crops to protect them from attacks by hosts of insects, snails, rodents, birds and mammals. Dr Howard gives some alarming insight into these toxins:

95% of these persistent man-made chemicals are ingested with the food we eat.

"Persistent" means that they accumulate in our fat cells and the body cannot break them down and detoxify them. They linger in our bodies and, even if excreted, they are simply recycled into the air, the water, the soil, and ultimately back into the food we eat. There is no place on earth, and no human being, that is not already contaminated. DDT is a classic example of this.

It was the Swedish Nobel Laureate Paul Muller who discovered in 1939 the potent insect-killing prowess of DDT, short for Dichloro-Diphenyl-Trichloroethane. It was only when Rachel Carson published her book *Silent Spring* in 1962 that the world woke up. The book records the damage done by the extensive and thoughtless use of this chemical.

The damage occurred before science was alerted to its potential toxicity and the impact it would have, not only on the targeted insect pests, but also on all their predators, birds and their chicks, fish and all aquatic life. DDT remains stored for life in the fatty tissues of humans and other animals. The higher the creature appears up the food chain, the greater the accumulation of toxic residues. We know that small fish are eaten by bigger fish, which are eaten in turn by even bigger fish,

while the fish are also eaten by birds and by people. So the amount of DDT per body weight increases.

James Clarke, in his book *Back to Earth: South Africa's Environmental Challenges*, talks about the concern that Rachel's death from cancer in 1964 sparked, especially since tests carried out in Johannesburg in that year revealed that "every man, woman and child had DDT in their adipose [fatty] tissue". One of the unfortunate side-effects of the DDT plague was that, once the damage had been done, the target pests often developed a resistance to the chemical and flourished as never before. There are many examples of this problem around the globe.

Dr Howard continues:

These potentially harmful chemicals are completely novel. Living systems can usually only efficiently detoxify chemicals found in the form and level to which the system has been exposed during its millions of years of evolution. Our systems have not had time to learn to cope with them.

At present agro-chemical manufacturers only have to prove that a new chemical is not harmful (using a battery of tests that are not exhaustive) before it is released into the environment. They do not have to show that the chemical is totally safe – which would be much harder to prove.

Most laboratory tests are performed on individual chemicals, acting alone, yet many may be used together to sort out more than one pest at a single application. Studies indicate that, in a "cocktail" of chemicals, any one chemical can be more powerful than any of the individual chemicals by themselves.

Some chemicals which have no ability to disrupt hormones by themselves, for example, might be capable of magnifying the ability of other chemicals to disrupt hormones. The fact that common industrial chemicals are interfering with hormones is a shocking one with far-reaching implications for many life forms, not least the higher animals.

For instance, some organo-chlorines (DDT is one of these) are key components of pesticides (and other consumer products). They are formed when chlorine combines with anything that has carbon in it, such as petroleum, sugar and carbohydrates, or as by-products of various industrial processes. When these organo-chlorines are ingested, they disrupt the finely-tuned human endocrine system, which uses hormones as messengers to control the workings of the body.

You may remember from biology classes during your school years how the endocrine system functions rather like a full orchestra, the conductor of which is the pituitary gland situated in the brain. If one musician strikes the wrong chord, the whole piece of music loses its harmony. In the human body, a malfunctioning hormonal system may lead to a legion of problems including birth deformities, breast and testicular cancer, infertility, neuro-behavioural defects in children, and poor memory, simply because each chemical messenger is responsible for certain aspects of the body's chemistry.

Although pesticide use has increased enormously since World War II, this has not meant that fewer crops are lost to insects. We're now losing over 20% more of our crops to insects alone than we were in the mid-1940s. What has actually happened is that insects have become increasingly resistant to pesticides while humans have not.

For those who extend their minds a little further, it leaves one feeling somewhat vulnerable in having to rely on other people and dwindling soil (and water) resources to produce our most basic needs. We need to question the way in which our food is grown, what is happening to our agricultural land, what is happening to our co-inhabitants on this planet, and what is happening to our personal and familial health and well-being.

Are we starting to get a glimpse of a possible future? Founder of the German Green Party, Petra Kelly, commented:

We, the generation that faces the next century, can add the solemn injunction, "If we don't do the impossible, we shall be faced with the unthinkable."

That's why we're posing the question: "Why organic?"

It seems to be the way out of "the unthinkable". In short, nature is robust.

Nature it has evolved over hundreds of millions of years and has resulted in a planet which is rich, with an enormous diversity of plants and animals, where all living things are interconnected in the most intricate ways. The threads in this vast web are strong and resilient. They have stood up to the tests of man for thousands of years. But is the web of the golden orb spider strong enough to withstand the passage of an elephant? Human beings are destroying the fragile links in the web of life at an alarming rate. When will it all collapse? We don't know the answer for sure. We can only surmise.

The British scientist James Lovelock in his book *The Revenge of Gaia* warns that many of the Earth's vital life-support systems may be on the brink of breakdown through human destruction of the planet's ecology. Without these systems, which provide essential oxygen, carbon dioxide, and temperature control, life will cease. This is what we have to bear in mind when we look at the question of "Why organic?"

Now read the heartfelt cry from Justus von Liebig, the inventor of chemical agriculture:

I have sinned against the wisdom of the creator and, justly, I have been punished. I wanted to improve his work because, in my blindness, I believed that a link in the astonishing chain of laws that govern and constantly renew life on the surface of the Earth had been forgotten. It seemed to me that weak and insignificant man had to redress this oversight.

Justus von Liebig wrote these words when reflecting on his life's work – that of producing chemical fertilisers from the wastes of war. He was hailed as the father of the Green Revolution which turned around food production after World War II. Agricultural lands produced bumper crops. It seemed that agriculture would never be the same again. Yet the tipping point came. We're now paying the price in exhausted and depleted soils around the world. Massive soil erosion attributed to loss of soil structure has reduced the amount of land available for crop production. Food production levels have dropped significantly despite the use of more and more chemical fertilisers, followed by the poisonous chemicals necessary to wipe out the pests and diseases attracted to stressed plants. Production costs have risen and farmers have started to look for ways of reducing input costs. They are returning to natural farming methods as a way of saving their bank balances, restoring their soils, producing better crops and being able to compete on local and international markets where discerning people are looking for foods which are grown according to the laws of nature, and which do not threaten their very existence on the planet.

How can we, as individuals, reduce the risks to our health and contribute towards the healing of our planetary home?

There is hope, and one simple solution.

Grow your own food.

Grow it the natural way.

Grow it following the instructions in this book.

If you follow all the guidelines for setting up a food garden, you're already on the road to harvesting your bounty – safe, fresh, delicious and nutritious, and plenty of it from a small patch of rich and healthy soil. You've already given yourself a new lease on life by experiencing the warmth of the sun on your skin, the wind in your hair, and the pleasure of pure physical exhaustion followed by deep, relaxed sleep.

In themselves, the feelings of well-being and happiness, fulfilment and self-worth created by working in harmony with Nature, and of experiencing the richness and tranquillity of your garden, are profoundly spiritual. Being with Nature is releasing, uplifting and healing. It is these experiences that add another dimension to the concept of "organic gardening" – holism, at its most whole.

Apart from anything else, growing your own food using simple, low-cost methods, using resources that are freely available, and conserving our precious and dwindling water supplies, gives many people the most important things of all: a true sense of purpose and an opportunity to use their own creativity to fashion what they need out of what they have.

Feed your body, your mind and your soul.

Go gardening with Nature.

Let it resonate in your heart, thoughts, feelings and actions.

The following chapters will give you some ways to feed and to occupy yourself that are inspiring and environmentally responsible.

Let us be the co-creators of a new world.

Let us all start with the soil.

So long as we feed on food from unhealthy soil, our spirit will lack the stamina to free itself from the prison of the body.

RUDOLF STEINER

CHAPTER TWO

What do you need to start a food garden?

The most important things are free…

- Lots of sunshine, water, and fresh air.
- Some basic information, the size of a seed. Water it, and it swells; nurture it, and it grows.
- Lots of enthusiasm, with a little hard work in the beginning.
- A pair of eyes, with hands attached.
- A small piece of ground – starting with as little as 20 square metres – to provide your family with something fresh every day.

If you do not have space, take a look at your existing garden beds. Introduce food plants to your herbaceous borders; plant them underneath shrubs and trees, around your roses, and on the pavement. And, if this is not possible, you can try growing vegetables in containers on your balcony, or outside the kitchen door (see Chapter 11). A little bit of fresh food from your very own garden is better than none at all.

Some things you can share or borrow…

- A spade, a garden fork, and a rake.
- If your soil is very hard, you may need a pick.
- Hand tools are also very useful.

If you must buy tools there are a few things to note:
- Buy the best quality tools you can afford. They are easier to use, and last for longer.

- Ladies' spades have a smaller head and are much easier on your back when digging.
- Metal buckets are heavier than plastic buckets, but they last longer.

If you cannot afford to buy new tools, watch out for auctions; take regular visits to second-hand and charity shops; or share with a neighbour or friend.

Some things are really nice to have but are not really that necessary...

- a hose pipe
- a watering can
- a wheelbarrow

Some things lie around waiting to be used...

- **old kitchen forks and spoons**, for transplanting seedlings; and
- **hard-plastic spray bottles**, for home-made insecticides or for a fine irrigation spray.

A little bit of effort and imagination will give you large rewards and loads of fun. Your vegetable garden could be the start of a great new life for you and your family.

You can save a lot of money by using rubbish to create:

- **a watering can** by punching small holes in the bottom of an old jam tin, or plastic bottle;
- **a shade-cloth** by cutting open plastic mesh bags (the type that vegetables are sold in) and sewing them together to form protective covers for your vegetable beds;
- **shade hats for single plants** by cutting out milk and juice containers;
- **a sled barrow** by cutting a drum in half, lengthwise, and nailing two long pieces of wood to the sides;
- **scoops for compost** by cutting out hard-plastic bottles;
- **a measuring stick** by using a straight piece of wood, one metre long and about 3 cm in width.

- Make lines across it with 5 cm gaps.
- Then mark the lines: 5, 10, 15, 20, 25, 30, 35, 40, 45, 50, 55, 60, 65, 70, 75, 80, 85, 90, 95.
- Make the 5s half a line in length, and the 10s a full line.

This stick can be used to measure out the length and width of a bed and to mark out the rows for seeds and seedlings.

- **A wooden dibber** for transplanting seedlings and to plant big seeds. Make your own from a broken spade or fork handle, or a piece of stick, cut to 30 cm and with the end shaved to a point.
- **A garden line** for marking lines and areas for digging. Make four sticks with sharpened points, one for each corner of the area you want to dig. You can then link them with a length of string.

> Treat yourself to something different!
>
> A magnifying glass (maybe two of different strengths) is great for watching the wildlife in your garden. You'll never go back to "soapies" on the box once you've spied on the little guys in the bushes. You'll also get some real inspiration for your creative activity from the patterns on insect egg shells and butterfly wings.

To be a successful food gardener, you will also need to understand your own health and that of your plants. Your needs – and their needs – must be met.

What do you need for good health?

Our good health requires a balanced diet, which consists of the essential nutrients in the correct proportions. Malnutrition (the "hidden hunger") arises when you get either an under- or over-supply of any of these nutrients. In other words, our daily food should provide us with the following:

- **Body-building foods** or proteins are used for building bones, muscles, skin, hair, blood and all your body organs.
- **Energy foods,** such as carbohydrates (starches and sugars), and fats and oils, provide the energy for growth and movement. Proteins may provide about 10 to 15 per cent of the energy needed by humans in developed countries. If you eat too much of them, the body converts them into fat, which is stored beneath the skin and around the internal organs.
- **Protective foods** have all the vitamins and minerals which are essential to good health. They build healthy immune systems and help the body to fight disease. When you are ill, they help you to recover. These vitamins and minerals are best found in fresh fruits and vegetables.

"Let food be your medicine;
let medicine be your food"
HIPPOCRATES

More and more medical research is showing us that fruit and vegetables protect us from coughs and colds and other infections, such as the bacteria that cause tuberculosis. Fresh fruit and vegetables protect us against the onset of many cancers; they prevent the thickening of arteries, a major cause of heart disease; they help prevent Alzheimer's, diabetes, anaemia, constipation, and so much more. Good food is our best medicine.

Yet many people do not know that fruit and vegetables protect us and that vegetables are even more important than fruit for good health. In order to be healthy, we have to eat a variety of fresh vegetables every day, especially the dark green leafy and yellow ones.

Don't think for one minute that vegetables provide us with vitamins and minerals only. They also give us the proteins, carbohydrates and oils we need for growth and development, the energy to live our lives fully, and the fibre required for a healthy digestive system.

What do plants need for healthy growth and development?

All living things, including you and green plants, have the same basic needs. These are: food, water, air, some form of protection against the elements, and care. Without any one of these, life is not possible. For survival, and for healthy growth and development, all these needs must be met.

- Plants obtain the nutrients (minerals) they require from soil. Directly or indirectly, all food comes from the soil.
- The sun provides the warmth and energy that plants need to grow. Inside their leaves, green plants use the sun's energy to grab the elements in ordinary water

and air. Together with the minerals they get through their roots from the soil, they make their own food, in a process called **photosynthesis**. Plans are thus the food factories of the world. They convert sunlight into a readily usable form of energy for all other living organisms. Just think about it. We are totally dependent on plant life for our survival, even if we were to eat meat alone, because animals also depend on plants for their food.

Green plants provide us with a lot of positive benefits:

- They produce the oxygen that we need to stay alive.
- They take out carbon dioxide from the atmosphere.
- Many of our medicines come from plants.
- They provide fibres for our clothing, timber for our furniture, paper to write on, and so much more.
- Plants also provide us with shelter and protection. A tree in your backyard gives you shade in summer, and helps to maintain an even temperature inside your house. Hedges may protect you against the prevailing winds and unwanted intruders.
- By making our world beautiful, they feed not only our bodies, but our souls as well.

Feed your soil well, and you will be well fed

As plants continue to grow, they take nutrients from the soil. If these minerals are not replaced by the normal cycles of nature, the soils will become less fertile. It then becomes the responsibility of the food gardener – the one who benefits from the harvest – to make sure that the soil maintains its fertility. All waste that comes from living things should be put into the soil to replace this lost food. This kind of waste is called **organic waste**.

Where does organic waste come from?

Look at your world with new eyes. We are far too hasty to throw things in the rubbish bin. There is a wealth of soil food in the stuff you normally throw away.

- Your **kitchen waste:** cabbage leaves, banana skins, orange peels, squash skins, peelings, egg shells, tea bags, coffee grounds and pot scrapings. Some of this "waste" is too valuable even to compost. Discarded parts of the turnip, radishes, carrot tops, and beetroot leaves should never be thrown away, because they make delicious and nutritious additions to the soup and stew pot. Turnip leaves are the richest source of Vitamin A of all the green vegetables.
- **Garden waste** (yours and your neighbours'): dead branches, weeds, the remains of harvested plants, fallen leaves, dead flowers and lawn clippings.
- Feathers, bones, egg boxes, cotton and wool rags, cardboard, paper, manure and old leather.

Organic waste is free: don't throw it away!

- **Start collecting as much organic waste as possible.** Ask your neighbours, your family and your friends to save their waste for your garden. They may think you're crazy, but just wait till they see what comes out of your well-fed soil. After turning green with envy, they will want to know how you did it.
- **Examine your rubbish with new eyes**, and make your own garden tools and equipment.

What else do you need to become a food gardener?

- **Knowledge comes from reading, looking, listening and thinking.**

Very often it means seeking out people who have experience and lots of skills. Pick their brains: ask hundreds of questions and never be afraid to experiment. We learn the most from the mistakes we make. And remember that there are many different ways of doing the same thing.

- **Understanding comes from thinking and questioning.**
  If things go wrong in the garden, don't just accept that it's happened. See if you can work out *why* it went wrong.

- **Consider what's working and what's not, so that changes can be made for the better.**
  Growing your own food is a whole new symphony of experiences. Slow yourself down and listen to the music of your garden. Gardening time is your opportunity to connect with yourself, with Nature and with the great Universal Energy.

- **Be prepared to talk to your plants!**
  In their book, *The Secret Life of Plants*, Peter Tompkins and Christopher Bird describe scientific research which shows how sensitive living plants really are, and how they interact with human beings.

One of the first people who studied scientifically how plants respond to human behaviour was the Indian physicist Sir Jagadis Chandra Bose, in the early part of the twentieth century. He discovered that plants go into severe shock when they are transplanted. This not only prevents them from settling in to their new situation, but the move also sets their growth right back. He went on to demonstrate that, by anaesthetising the plants before they were transplanted, they took to their new environment immediately.

Scientists have also shown that plants are sensitive even to human thoughts. Now we know that plants need to be treated with care and consideration: we need to show them gratitude for all that they do for us.

Have a vision, then, not just of a beautiful and bountiful food garden, but of people coming together; not just "growing cabbages, but souls" – and look after your soul first.

When you blow your breath on a cold window pane, the frost that appears is part of you, just as the plants we "feed" with our radiations are part of us. We are, in fact, all part of one thing, all materialisations of the one life.

THE FINDHORN COMMUNITY

CHAPTER THREE

Planning your garden and preparing your body

Think before you dig

Because a food garden is an investment in your future good health and well-being, you need to sit down with a pencil and paper and really think. Before you design your garden layout, here are some planning tips:

- Make sure that your crops have what they need:
- lots of sunshine (at least six hours in the early part of the day);
  - enough water;
  - plenty of fresh air circulating around them;
  - fertile soil; and
  - protection from the wind.

Last, but not least – because you will have to care for the garden yourself – you will need to be able to get to it easily. Try to make it close to the kitchen. If it is out of sight and out of mind, a lot of problems will creep in.

- **Where does the sun rise and set? How much sun does each part of your garden get during the day?** Remember that buildings, trees and hedges cast shadows and that shadows are longer in winter.
- **Where do you live? What type of climate do you have? Do you have rainy winters and dry summers, or the other way round? Do you have frost in winter? Are you near the coast where the moisture in the air is high?**

- **If your garden is on a slope,** you will have to either terrace it or build shallow ditches to slow down the water run-off. These terraces and ditches also help to sink the water into the ground without losing your precious topsoil.
- **What plants do you see in your neighbourhood that are doing well?** Talk to your friends and neighbours about their food-growing successes and failures. They will be happy to tell you about local challenges and which plants will thrive.
- **Find out from what direction the common winds arrive in your area.** For example: in South Africa's Cape Peninsula, summer brings the howling south-easter and winter is characterised by a north-westerly wind. Both are damaging to plants.
- **During the rainy season, will the water stand on top of the soil and deny air to the roots?** This is also known as a drainage problem and may be caused either by your soil type (clay soils tend to hold water) or by the fact that there is no slope to allow the right amount of run-off.
- **You may find different soil types in your garden.** What type of soil do you have? It may be a good idea to have a soil test done before you start. Try and site your food garden where you have the best soil. You can improve even the poorest soil by working in lots of compost and well-rotted manure.

- **Do you have large trees, shrubs and hedges nearby?** Their roots should not extend too far into your garden, because they will compete with your crops for nutrients and water.
- **How much space do you have?** Is your garden big enough to include fruit trees, climbing vines and sprawling vegetables?

Windbreak from shrubs and bushes

Calculating the direction of the wind

- Take a one-metre length of toilet paper and stand outside the area you want to turn into a garden when the wind is blowing.
- Hold the toilet paper at one end and let the rest blow away from you.
- The line of the flapping toilet paper, from the free end to the end in your hand, will tell you where the wind is coming from.
- The hand that holds your end of the paper will also point towards those areas of your garden which will bear the biggest impact of that wind and which will therefore suffer the worst damage.
- Place or plant a wind break between that place and the face of the wind.

Calculating wind direction

- **Do you have space that you can allocate specifically for a food garden, or will you grow food among your ordinary garden plants or in containers?**
- **Is your garden walled or fenced?** Will you be troubled by wandering dogs, porcupines, baboons, goats and cows, chickens, geese or guinea fowl? What about other intruders?
- **Where are your water points?** A tap near the garden makes your life easier.
- **When it comes to choosing your vegetables and fruit,** ask yourself: what do you and your family really like eating, and what should you be eating, for radiant health? Your own food garden may give you the chance to try fruits and vegetables that you have never tried before.
- **Are you going to plant herbs, flowers and trees?** Are you going to have a dedicated area for culinary and medicinal plants, or are you going to grow your entire garden for body, mind and soul? In this chapter, you will find tips on what you might plant to give you the effect and results that you want.

- **What features are you going to include in your garden?**

  - compost heaps or bins
  - earthworm farms
  - a chicken coop
  - a pond
  - a bird bath
  - a herb garden
  - an orchard

  - a nursery to raise your own seedlings and plants
  - a bench on which you can rest and contemplate your creation in partnership with Nature and where you can listen to the birds and the bees, and the frogs and the trees
  - apart from wind breaks, mentioned above, you may also want to create trellised walkways for vines

How to measure the height of a tree, building or hedge

Remember that vegetables need at least six hours of full sun every day. When you are looking for the right place for your vegetable patch, watch out for anything that might throw a shadow across your food garden (an obstacle).

- Choose the obstacle that you want to measure.
- Turn your back and walk away from the obstacle.
- Stop and place your feet about 50 cm apart.
- Bend down and place your hands on the ground.
- Look back through your legs and see if you can see the obstacle.

- If you cannot see the top of the obstacle, move further away and try again until you can.
- When you can just see the top of the obstacle, stand up.
- Measure the distance back to the tree by pacing it out and this will give you its height. One stride equals about one metre.
- Check your stride against your spade.

This little exercise will also give you an indication of how flexible your body is!

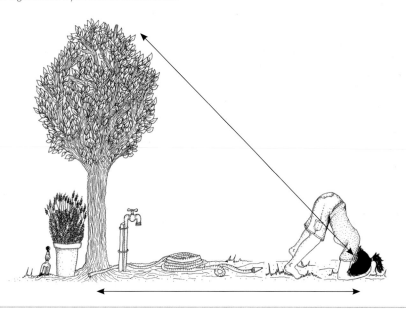

Once you have thought about all these points, create a list of all the features you need to include in your garden. Then draw up a plan on a piece of graph paper and work out where you want to place things in relation to each other. Draw things to scale so that your plan is realistic.

Imagine you are a bird flying overhead, looking down on what you have in mind. It doesn't matter whether you are starting a new garden, revamping an existing garden, or simply changing your gardening habits and going the organic route: this is an extremely valuable exercise and will probably take you a fair amount of time.

When designing your garden, don't be afraid to exercise your creative skills. Never doubt your own innate ability to turn a bare piece of land into a beautiful, bountiful place which will feed your body, your mind and your soul.

To sum up, here is the ideal place for a food garden:

- Close to the kitchen, or where you can see it and take care of it. Out of sight, out of mind.
- Near a tap or other source of water.
- Stay away from large trees and hedges.
- Keep the food garden protected from the wind.
- Plant your vegetables where the soil in your garden is best.

When gardeners garden, it is not just the plants that grow, but the gardeners themselves.
KEN DRUSE

Preparing the site

Once you have chosen the site and finished the layout, you may have to remove grass, bushes, trees and their roots. Keep all this plant material for composting, mulching and filling trench beds or putting into the compost heap. Get rid of materials that you cannot re-use elsewhere (buried building materials, glass, old timber – it is amazing what you find when you start digging) and put rocks and other useful objects to one side for later use. Rocks, for instance, can be used for landscaping a pond area or for building a rockery for herbs.

Laying out the garden

When you start to lay out your garden plot, you need to bear four points in mind:

1 If your plot is on a slope, the length (or long axis) of the beds should always be across the slope. This slows the water down and stops it from washing the soil away.

2 If it is possible, the long axis of the beds should run from east to west.

3 The width of the beds should never be more than one metre.

4 Always work in the garden from the pathways. That way the soil in the beds is never trampled and compacted. Pathways should be about half a metre in width.

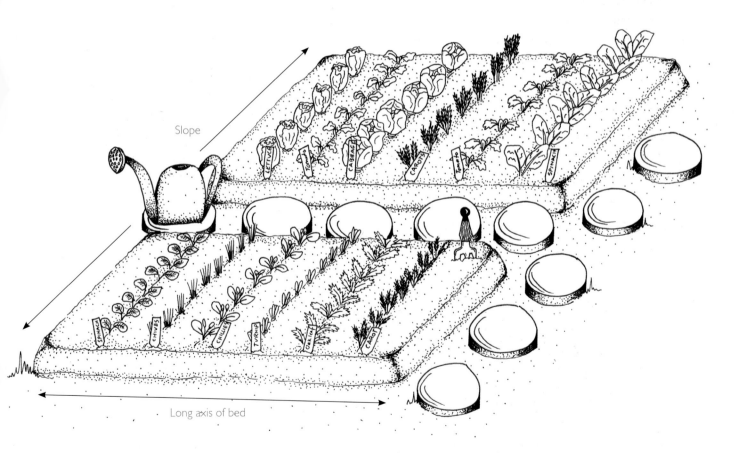

Slope

Long axis of bed

If your plot is on a slope, the long axis of the bed should run at tight angles to it.

Using a measuring stick and garden lines, or a spade, mark out the beds. A good size for each bed is one metre (or one spade) wide by two or three metres (or spades) long. Mark the corners of the beds with stakes. The pathways between the beds should be no more than a half-metre wide.

Marking out a door-sized bed

If you want curved beds, the same principles apply (see opposite page).

Once your garden is marked out, start preparing the soil in the beds for planting.

It is always better to make separate beds in the garden – never just one big bed. You'll see the merit in this once you have done the really hard work of preparing the soil.

Planting ideas – culinary and medicinal

Spend some time on research

Many books are available in bookshops and libraries that will give you an insight into the exciting world of food plants. Don't be tempted to stick with the tried and tested varieties. Experiment with colours, textures, tastes and smells. Remember: the more you eat a variety of different foods each day, the more likely you will get the essential nutrients for optimum health.

Plant roots seek out diverse minerals in the soil. Some plants send their feeder roots deep into the bowels of the earth, others feed at the surface. All take up different materials for their various needs. Also look at plants as visual and structural elements in your garden. Find out:

- Are their root systems shallow, deep or spreading?
- How tall will the plants grow?
- How large are their canopies?
- Will they tolerate partial shade, wind and frost?
- When will they produce flowers?
- Will they give you a colourful display?
- When can you harvest the fruits of your labour?

The more you know about their growth habits and needs before you start planting, the more likely you will be a successful food gardener.

1. Picture the outline of your curved bed in your mind.

2. Bend a length of hosepipe on the ground to create the outline you want.

3. Sprinkle lime or river sand along the side of the hose.

4. Take the hose away and dig along the line of lime or sand.

Marking out curved bed using a hosepipe and sand

Here is a selection of plants (both medicinal and culinary, indigenous and exotic, and many more multipurpose plants) that I have sorted into various categories for convenience. It is by no means an exhaustive list, but it's a start.

Herbs for tasty cooking and for healing

Sorrel, rosemary, lavender, marjoram, oregano, basil, bergamot, lemon balm, lovage, hyssop, coriander (dhanya), fennel, bay, tarragon, borage, caraway, angelica, chervil, chives, dill, mint varieties, chamomile, sage, thyme, yarrow, ginger, chillies, wild ginger, Vietnamese coriander, pennywort, *wilde als*, rocket, water cress, land cress, parsley (curly and Italian), purslane, salad burnet, wild rosemary, pineapple.

Pest-repelling plants

Wilde als, wormwood, southern wood, feverfew, fennel, rosemary, lavender, rue, marigolds, garlic, chives, basil, garlic chives, tomatoes, onions, most herbs.

Colourful plants

Jerusalem artichokes, calendula, marigold, day lilies, ornamental and curly kale, chillies, sunflowers, pineapple, sage, nasturtium, agapanthus, Bright Lights Swiss chard.

Compost activators

Comfrey, yarrow, dandelions, elderberry.

Soil builders

Peas, beans, broad beans, chick peas, lentils, lucerne, soya beans, lupins, yarrow, comfrey.

Speciality plants for the kitchen

Asparagus, globe artichokes, Jerusalem artichokes, Chinese and Japanese vegetables, kohlrabi, parsnips, chicory, endives, all sorts of salad leaves, Brussels sprouts, garlic, elephant garlic, shallots, broad beans, African horned cucumber.

Comfrey

Food trees

Lemon, almond, orange, grapefruit, plum, apricot, fig, nectarine, banana, tree tomato, plums, pears, apples, carob, drumstick tree, elderberry, kumquat, loquat, peach, quince, fig, grapefruit, Kei apple, marula, *waterbessie*, naartjie, paw-paw.

Vines and climbing plants

Grapes, granadilla, cucumbers, seven-year beans, asparagus (yard-long) beans, peas, blackberries, raspberries, chayote (chou marrow or sou sou).

Creeping plants and ground covers

(need a lot of horizontal space)

Pumpkins, gem squash, butternut, New Zealand spinach,

strawberries, melons, chayote (chou marrow or sou sou), *vroubossie* (carpet geranium), *impepho*.

Fragrant plants

Bergamot, lemon balm, lemon- and rose-scented pelargonium, buchu species.

Edible flowers

Calendula, carnation, carpet geraniums, bulbine, dandelion, elderflowers, radish, rocket, nasturtium, rose, wild garlic, borage, violas, globe artichokes, Cape sorrel, chamomile, day lilies, pineapple sage, cucurbit flowers, *waterblommetjie* (except that they only grow in water!).

Succulents and aloes

Aloe ferox and *Aloe vera*, *vygie*, pig's ear, *spekboom*.

Vegetables

(see planting guide on pages 174–6 for a list of the most commonly planted vegetables)
Fancy lettuce varieties, water cress, land cress, endive, Florence fennel, rhubarb, peanuts, parsnips, celeriac, Brussels sprouts, okra, shallots, amaranth, *merogo*, Chinese and Japanese greens, red cabbage, Savoy cabbage, endive, chicory, taro, yams, soya beans, Jerusalem artichokes, corn salad, rhubarb, amaranthus, *waterblommetjie*, purslane.

Shrubs and perennials

Cape gooseberry, blackberries, youngberries, raspberries.

And now for the hard work!
Digging can be a back-breaker.
So prepare yourself well in advance.

Yarrow flowers

Rue flowers

Preparing your body for digging, composting and planting

Since a healthy organic garden cannot do without good soil, you will find that it is worth the time and effort to do the job well. Because this work may push you to the limits of your physical prowess, you will need to prepare yourself in advance. Exercise gently every day to strengthen the muscles you'll be using. Here are a few ideas to get those muscles loose and supple, particularly in your back, shoulders and legs.

Shoulder rolls

Gently and slowly roll your shoulders five times forward and five times backward.

Supple back

Place your feet apart in line with your shoulders. Gently reach up with your right arm, and squeeze your fist over your head. At the same time, drop your left hand to your side. Slowly count to five, while you feel the muscles stretching all the way down the right side of your body.

Repeat the process with your left arm up and your right arm down. This exercise will help to make your back supple. Hold for a slow count of ten on each side. Breathe deeply all the time as you "reach for the stars". Repeat the exercise five times for each arm.

Head rolls

Drop your head forward so that your chin touches your chest and gently and slowly roll it from side to side, and around the clock. If you have neck problems, only roll from side to side.

"Around the world"

Hold your arms straight out at right angles to your sides. Place your feet apart and bend slightly forward at the waist. Keeping your upper back straight, gently swing your arms to the front and back, each arm moving through 180°. Repeat up to 15 times. One circle equals one count.

Squatting

Lean your back against the wall. Slide slowly downwards into a sitting position as if you were on an imaginary chair. Count to ten, relax and repeat another five times.

Lower back and thighs

Lie flat with your back pressed onto the floor or bed, legs extended. Draw one leg into a "knee-up" position and hold it to your chest. Repeat five times and then do it with the other leg. With your back still flat on the floor and with your knees bent, tighten your bum muscles and hold for a count of ten. Relax. Repeat five times. Tighten your tummy muscles at the same time.

Leg stretch

Put one foot behind the other and slowly reach down to the ground while keeping the back foot on the ground. Hold this stretch for a slow count of twenty, then put the other foot back and bring the back one forward. Stretch again, while you count to twenty. Repeat five or six times, and slowly increase the number of stretches over a period of days to really work those muscles. Breathe deeply while you do it.

Deep knee bends

Place one hand on a spade, or some other support like a fence or a chair. Slowly squat all the way down, then slowly slide up. Legs should be angled to the sides for more stretch in the groin area. Start with five repetitions and try to work up the number of squats as your muscles strengthen.

Remember that your mind may be geared up for gardening, but – if you haven't prepared your muscles – you are bound to suffer a lot of aches and pains. And while we're about it, never tackle a whole day in the garden if you're not used to exercise. Rather start off with an hour or two, and slowly build up the time you spend with spade and rake in hand.

Now you are ready!

Pick up your spade, and get digging. If you start to flag, remember that you're in this for really good reasons:

- Growing your own food is one of the most important activities you will ever do. You will discover the world around you, and something about yourself.

- Apart from a fresh, tasty and nutritious addition to your diet, think of the boost to your immune system. Fresh air, sunshine, exercise, and relaxation: all help to strengthen your body's ability to fight disease.

- While you're out there, what are you thinking about? Certainly not about your problems. You're focusing on what you're doing; living in the now. It's a kind of meditation. And what's more, it's taking you right to the core of Nature, where it's all happening right in front of your eyes. The more you do it, the more you observe and learn, and the greater your passion for the journey you're on.

- You have a new sense of purpose, and always something exciting to do. Every day is a new day. Every day exposes another of Mother Nature's secrets. Get out there, and use your senses to the full.

- You're making a difference – to your health and that of your family, and to the health of the planet. For one thing (and you'll find there are many others), when you get rid of your household and garden waste in the ways that you find in this book, you will be helping to create a better future for all. Do you want to know how and why? Look at Chapter 6 on earthworm farming. You will find that adding more organic matter to the soils of Planet Earth can take the sting out of global warming.

- In any event, you are bound to find your own reasons for being out there. One thing is for sure: food gardening is addictive, and it's one way to meet people and make friends. There is always something to talk about and it's really interesting stuff.

And so, to end this chapter, here is a story.

... the gardener rose from nowhere, wearing leather sandals and carrying a long oak staff.

- He wandered through the squares and market looking for ... a spacious piece of land. Eventually he found a place near a sparkling golden stream.
- He built a hut and around it a garden, as big as the trails of wind, bordered by ivy, clematis, passionflowers and honeysuckle, and dotted with lilies, violets, irises and pansies.
- He sat by the entrance to the garden, offering its peace and beauty to all who wished to take pleasure from it. He told them it was the garden of life, and all those who wished to find peace in it would always find the door open.

- Birds and squirrels made their nests in the trees, fairies and elves looked for shelter among its plants, and men found refuge among the flowers.
- And the gardener devoted himself to the care of plants and trees, squirrels and birds, fairies, elves and men. (From *The Gardener*)

CHAPTER FOUR

CHAPTER FOUR

Understanding your soil and your plant nutrition

Soil: our most precious resource

Dr Gert van der Linde is Director of the Fertiliser Society of South Africa. He says that, although we know that the nutrients in food are important for our health, global food systems do not provide enough of those essential nutrients. A global health study published in 2002, for example, reported that around 23 million deaths throughout the world could be related to poor diets. Dr van der Linde says that we need at least fifty nutrients to live healthy, productive lives. The small amount of these nutrients that we need, compared to the rest of our diet, is very small: as little as a few parts per million. So it is hard to believe that we suffer from poor diets. Yet, when we look at the least amounts needed (such as iron, iodine, selenium, zinc, vitamin A, and others), we find that a shortage in the diet of these nutrients afflicts over half the world's population, or three billion people. A lack of iron in people's diets, for example, rose from about 35% of the world's population in 1960 to 50% in 2000.

Our concern grows bigger when we read of the sickness of this beautiful planet on which we live, this little sphere of rock put together from the dust of ancient stars. When the first astronauts circled the Earth in their space craft, they said it looked like a blue pearl in space. That outer shell of the planet, where all creatures can live, is called the biosphere. Taken together with the upper layer of air, it provides a very fragile film around the planet, separating its surface from the vast vacuum of space.

The soil, which forms the foundation of the biosphere, covers about one third of our planet's land surface. It is one of our most precious natural resources. Without the soil and its legions of microbes, there would be no life. How many of us understand its critical role in our health and well-being, and in the very future of life as we know it on Earth? How many are aware that a mere twenty centimetres of topsoil is all that separates mankind from starvation? Yet, each year, a huge chunk of agricultural land is lost to erosion, the build-up of salts, the rise of concrete jungles, and other forms of degradation.

Soil erosion and soil fertility

Throughout the world, the bulk of all food production depends on good soils. In South Africa, less than 14% of the land surface can be used for agriculture, and much of this land has been severely degraded by soil erosion. Scientists estimate that our annual loss of soil is between 300 and 400 million tonnes.

Under natural conditions, soil increases at a rate of 0,2 to 0,3 tonnes per hectare per year, or 1 mm of soil per hectare every 100 to 400 years. If human activities, agriculture or natural disasters strip out the natural plant cover, the rate of soil loss can speed up to as much as 30 tonnes per hectare a year.

The ever-thinning layers of soil that cover the land masses are in a sorry state. For much of the twentieth century, poor farming methods have overworked the soils. Greedy business interests tried to boost crop production by the heavy use of artificial fertilisers and poisonous chemicals.

Alexis Carrel – Nobel Prize winner and author of the classic *Man, the Unknown* – warned in 1912 of the consequences to our health of growing our food on tired and depleted soils. "Directly, or indirectly," he said, "all food comes from the soil. All of life will be healthy, or unhealthy, according to the fertility of the soil."

In other words:

healthy soil = healthy plants = healthy people

Many scientific studies have tried to destroy the claims of organic farmers that their produce has a higher nutritional value. Yet these studies have simply proved that it is worth eating food grown in healthy soils. Even guinea pigs at the German Federal Institute for Consumer Health Protection, when given a choice of conventional and organic carrots, selected the organic produce!

On a higher level of spiritual insight, Christian mystic Rudolf Steiner said that "so long as we feed on food from unhealthy soil, our spirit will lack the stamina to free itself from the prison of the body".

These are sobering thoughts, and – if we extend our thoughts a little further – it leaves us feeling somewhat vulnerable. We see that we have to rely on other people and dwindling soil resources to produce our most basic needs. For many of us, the rising cost of all foods, especially vegetables, makes it difficult to eat something fresh and green every day.

Take action to improve your patch

So, the best way of cutting costs – and of taking responsibility for your own health – is to spend a few rands on a spade and some seeds, and reap the benefits of fresh, safe and nutritious produce from your own home garden. Even with a very small piece of land, you can grow a large quantity and variety of vegetables by practising the simple, low-cost methods outlined in this book.

What's more, the tried and tested techniques in this book will not only save water, but help to reduce the effect that you and your household have on the waste stream of the city, town or village where you live. Slowly you will become aware of the rubbish that your household generates.

More than half of your household rubbish is actually

Loss of soil through human activity (erosion)

really good food for the soil. You can turn that rubbish into a beautiful, rich part of soil called humus. This stuff not only helps to hold water in the soil, but also holds the soil particles together and so prevents erosion by wind and water, and actively promotes healthy plant growth.

By working to restore harmony to the soil, by good soil-building practices, we are working towards good health for all. The late Marie Roux, formerly of Operation Grow and author of *Grow to Live*, taught the communities in which she worked: "There is an inextricable connection between soil, nutrition and human health." To put it simply: you are what you eat.

Grab a handful of soil

Besides supplying nutrients that plants need for healthy growth, soil also provides room for root growth to "hold up the plant", along with air and water, which are essential for life. In their physical nature and water-holding capacity soils vary a great deal.

Take a walk around your neighbourhood or your own garden. Take a handful of soil from here and there, and compare the colour and texture of the different samples. Some are heavy and firm, with small particles; others are light and loose, with larger ones. You will find clay soils, sandy soils, loams and many variations in between. You will find that you can work them more easily or with difficulty. They will have different nutrient levels, different drainage and allow different kinds of plants to grow on them. Each soil has to be treated in its own way to make it more suitable for gardening purposes.

What we're interested in is the ability of a soil type to hold water, because this is the critical issue in our semi-arid country. Some soils hold water well; others don't. Two of the reasons for this are:

- Particle size: The smallest bits of water are called molecules. Only if they attach themselves to the smallest particles of soil do they become available to plant roots. If the water molecules lie in the spaces *between* soil particles, they are <u>not</u> available to the roots. Sandy soils are mostly made up of larger particles, while clayey soils have a lot more smaller particles. The figure on page 37 gives an idea of the different water-holding capacities of the two.
- The amount of organic matter in the soil and, therefore, the amount of humus.

Before we look at humus, however, we need a basic understanding of the world of soil.

What is soil?

The patch of "dirt" outside your back door has a story to tell: one that goes back millions of years. It took a long, long time to acquire the status of being dirt. And it's not simply something to hold plants upright in your garden. There's a whole lot more to it than that.

First of all, where did the dirt come from?

Millions of years of temperature extremes cracked the great rock that was earth. Rocks broke into stones, stones into pebbles and pebbles into grit. Cascading water, gliding glaciers and unrelenting winds carried the ever-smaller chunks over vast distances, grinding them against one another and breaking them up even further.

Soil thus came from the **weathering** or disintegration of the earth's crust – rather like when you crumble bread to feed the ducks. The mineral particles that result from all this weathering are of different sizes and they all make up the non-living (or **inorganic**) parts of soil.

But soil is more than mineral particles.

When living matter gives off waste products and finally dies, the waste and dead remains are broken down into humus by the teeming microbes and other life forms. These make up the **organic** matter in the soil. Air and water are also vital in maintaining the cycle of soil life.

Everything works together to form this precious resource on which all human life depends. So, all citizens of the earth have to ensure the integrity and fertility of our soils. After all, there is only about four percent of our planet that we need for food production. This very same soil that has been destroyed by conventional farming and gardening methods has been polluted by technology and industry and by our continued use of hazardous chemicals.

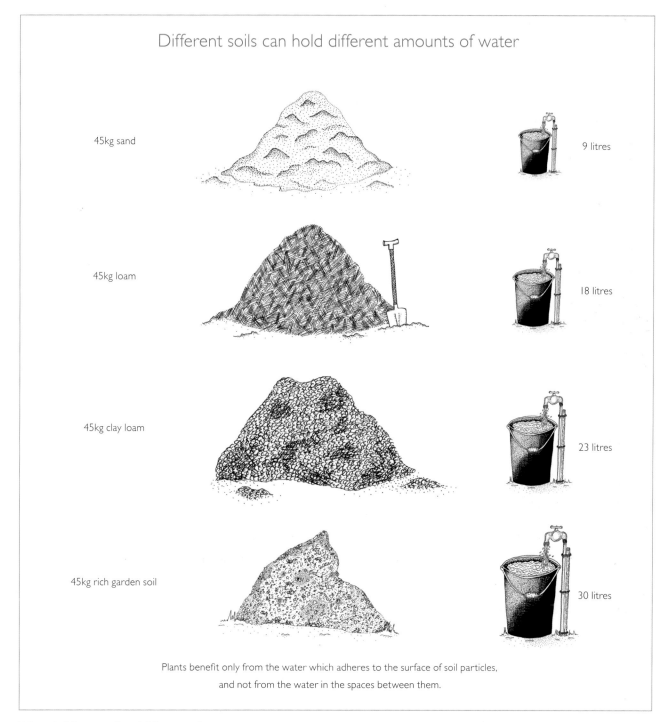

Different soils can hold different amounts of water

45kg sand — 9 litres

45kg loam — 18 litres

45kg clay loam — 23 litres

45kg rich garden soil — 30 litres

Plants benefit only from the water which adheres to the surface of soil particles,
and not from the water in the spaces between them.

Water-holding capacity of different soils

What the average soil is made of

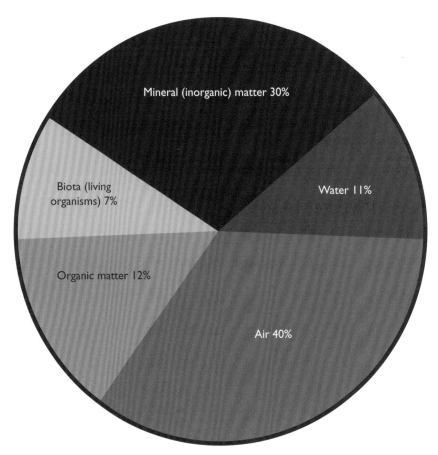

Source: *Permaculture: A Designer's Manual*, by Bill Mollison

Of course, this will vary depending on the soil type, and there will substantial differences between topsoil and subsoil. Also, in dry climates, the organic component is much reduced and may be as little as one per cent. Air and water percentages will depend on the water status of the soil, which in turn is influenced by texture.

There are many different types of soils

Gardeners need to know what makes for the best kind of soil when it comes to growing fruit, vegetables and herbs.

The size of the soil particles and the amount of humus present are the most important features to look at. They give an indication of soil fertility, because they both affect the size of the air spaces between the particles and therefore tell you how much water the soil can hold.

Soils can be separated into three main types. Rubbing samples between your fingers will give you some idea of particle size and texture.

Soil type	Features	Meaning	Ways to improve	Suitable crops
Sand	• Mainly large particles with big spaces between them. (Generally consist of more than 80% coarse and fine sand particles.) • Usually light in colour.	• Well-aerated, and good drainage which means no water-logging in the rainy season. Also dries out very quickly after watering, leaches minerals out easily, so nutrient levels are generally low. Less water is lost to evaporation at the surface and soils tend to be warmer. • Very little organic matter and therefore little, or no, humus. Poor fertility. Light and easy to work because sandy particles do not stick together. Plant roots can grow easily in sandy soil. Easily washed or blown away, which leads to loss of valuable topsoil.	• Regularly add organic matter, using one of the ways shown in Chapter 5. • Use green manure crops and dig them in when they are young and tender. Add some older manure at the same time to make up for a loss of nitrogen, which is used up as the green manure decomposes.	• All root crops: carrots, turnips, parsnips, radishes, onions, sweet potatoes, potatoes, groundnuts, beetroot, sugar beet.
Clay	• Made up of very fine particles and has a fine, smooth texture. (Made up of more than 90% very fine silt or clay particles and less than 10% larger sand particles.)	• Small particles mean small airspaces, which hold very little air. • Small particles attract many mineral ions. Nutrient content high.	• Regularly add organic matter in one of the ways described in Chapter 5. • Constantly dig in compost.	• Trees with strong root systems. • Plants with strong root systems like lucerne.

Soil type	Features	Meaning	Ways to improve	Suitable crops
Clay	• Small airspaces between particles. • Particles aggregate together to form clods. • Fairly dark in colour.	• Poor aeration. • Water seeps very slowly through the small air-spaces. Drainage is therefore poor, but water retention is very good. Can get water-logged in rainy season. • Particles stick together tightly when wet, which makes a heavy soil, hard to work. • Does not erode easily. • Retained water evaporates easily from the surface. Tend to be cold soils. • A heavy soil, hard to work especially when dry. • Retains organic matter and, therefore, humus levels are high. A fertile soil.	• Use gypsum to improve crumb structure.	• In lighter clay soils you can grow crops like tomatoes and beans although most plants will grow more slowly. Root crops do not do well as they cannot penetrate the soil.
Loam (silt)	• Regarded as being the best soil for most crop plants. • Particles vary in size; roughly 30% fine clay particles, and up to 30% sand particles. • The properties of loam soils are intermediate between those of sand and clay.	• Generally well-aerated. • Well-drained and does not easily waterlog. • Holds water well and does not dry out quickly. • Easy to work. • Good fertility.	• Regularly add organic matter.	• All crops can be planted.

What is humus, and where does it come from?

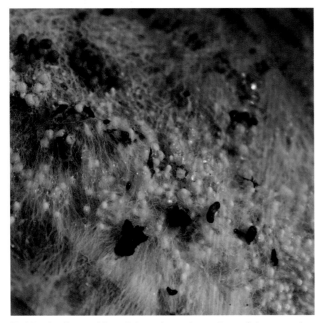

Fruiting bodies and fungal threads on the surface of decomposing organic matter

First and foremost, soil is a living system. Millions of tiny micro-organisms live out their lives in the soil and take their nutrients and energy from proteins, carbohydrates, lipids and minerals that are normally in their environment.

Within the soil these microbes reproduce at amazing rates. A single bacterium can reach maturity and divide in less than half an hour. In the course of a single day, they can make 300 million more of themselves. During the second day, they can produce more of themselves than the number of human beings that have ever lived.

Like any life form, however, they cannot survive and reproduce without food, air and water. Their food is dead vegetable matter (like old dead leaves, the remains of crops, leaf mould, lawn clippings) and the dead remains of animals or their waste products (such as manure and urine). This is what microbes convert into humus – a brown or black sticky substance, produced by the decomposition of plant and animal materials under proper environmental and biological conditions.

When soils are lacking in humus, though they may be rich in other respects, they are no more productive than pure sand. Humus makes all soils more mellow and friable, and more suitable for growing plants. Humus can absorb many times its own weight in water and, for this reason, it improves poor, sandy soils and makes them more productive by increasing the soil's ability to hold water.

The best soils consist of various texture groups (sand, silt, clay *and* organic matter) with the soil particles clumping together in aggregates or "crumbs". Humus works as a kind of cement to stick soil particles together and keep them in place. The simplest life forms, or organisms, that live in the soil also play an important part.

For example: the white threads of moulds help to bundle soil particles into clumps, while earthworms "eat" soil and form aggregates inside their bodies, which they then pass out as castings. This crumb structure creates pores of various sizes – fine pores (which hold water and dissolved nutrients) and large pores between the 'crumbs' (which enable water to pass out quickly and therefore remain filled with air).

This explains why, in the figure on page 37, the "rich" garden soil holds more water than the other soil types. Soil aggregates provide roots with essential air, water and nutrients. The presence of humus is an indication of soil vitality and soil fertility. It is perhaps one of the most important constituents of a healthy soil, yet most of our soils are lacking it.

Sadly, most arable soils around the world are no longer "alive". Living organisms cannot survive the onslaught of chemical cocktails, compaction and the damage caused by heavy machinery, and the lack of food in the form of organic waste. If soil is not alive, it is not going to support the plants that you're attempting to grow. It will not have the nutrients on tap; there will be insufficient air to support living root systems to sustain healthy plant growth; it will not retain the water that is so vital for growth and development.

Why harp on about humus? Go back to the problem of water. South Africa is the 27th most arid country in the world and the situation promises to get worse. What are we going to do about it?

Create humus, of course

There are many ways to create a humus-rich soil. Either you can dig a variety of un-decomposed organic material

Sticky, black humus

directly into the soil (by trenching and double digging) or you can dig in large amounts of organic compost (home-made preferably). You can also work the soil from the top by mulching. This book includes a number of methods for increasing the organic matter in soil, and thereby providing essential humus. These include trenching, double digging, sheet mulching, composting, vermi-culture and making plants work for you.

Prepare your soil thoroughly and provide a good layer of mulch. Then the action of rain and the work of an amazing variety of soil life over time will turn the organic matter you have introduced into your soil into a rich, brown, loamy humus.

This awesome substance literally changes your soil into gold dust:

- It holds water and nutrients and releases them on demand.

- It prevents the leaching of valuable plant foods from the soil.

- It sticks soil particles together and prevents them from blowing and washing away.

- It makes the soil light and fluffy for good root growth. Vigorous root systems are essential for strong and healthy plants.

The answer to all your problems, now and in the future, is to feed your soil with all your waste. If you have any doubt whether your domestic waste is really soil food, ask yourself these questions: "Was it once alive?" and "Will it rot?" If the answer to these questions is "Yes", then bury it, mulch with it, add it to the compost heap, feed the worms and create –

life-giving, water-saving, nutrient-catching
HUMUS.

Food for plants

We looked briefly at how soil is produced by the weathering of the earth's rocky crust, which produces soil particles of all different shapes and sizes. The weathering process doesn't end here. It goes on and on, the particles being broken down into even smaller particles, which we call **mineral salts**. These make up the plant nutrients, some of which you may know after seeing them in packets on supermarket shelves and in garden shops. They are used to boost plant growth in tired and depleted soils. Healthy soils will provide sufficient quantities of all the essential nutrients and the plants will not show signs and symptoms of deficiencies.

What are the nutrients that healthy soils provide?

There are 16 essential nutrients for healthy plant growth and development. Thirteen of them come from the soil and three (carbon, hydrogen and oxygen) are obtained from air and water.

Of the 13 soil nutrients, there are the macro-nutrients which are required in larger amounts. These are: nitrogen, phosphorus and potassium (these three are needed by the plants in large amounts), and calcium and magnesium (which the plants need in smaller amounts).

The **trace elements**, or **micro-nutrients**, are used in very tiny amounts and are found in most soils. They are: boron, chlorine, copper, iron, manganese, molybdenum, sulphur and zinc.

A basic plant-nutrient deficiency chart

Generally, plants show less well-defined symptoms in the garden itself. What you will notice, however, is that plant growth and yields will be affected. If your plants are showing signs of deficiencies, first of all check the pH, because if the soil is too acid or alkaline, the plant roots are unable to take up various minerals. The term pH is often used to describe the degree of acidity (sourness) or alkalinity. For example, a more acid solution would be described as having a lower pH, and a less acid, or more alkaline, solution as having a higher pH.

A scale (from 1 to 14) is used in referring to pH values. On this scale, a pH of 7 means neutral (neither acid nor alkaline), with pH 6, 5, 4 ... being more and more acidic (0 is the most acidic), while pH values of 8, 9, 10 ... indicate increasing alkalinity (14 is the most strongly alkaline).

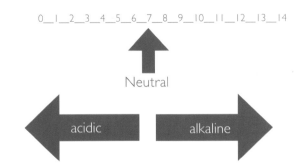

pH scale:

0__1__2__3__4__5__6__7__8__9__10__11__12__13__14

Neutral

acidic   alkaline

A measure of acidity and alkalinity

Most garden shops sell simple pH meters. A soil test will give you a more accurate picture and show you whether it is only the pH that needs altering or whether there is a lack of specific nutrients as well.

You can test the pH of your soil by using pH indicator paper, available at most chemists. This paper changes colour, depending on the pH of the solution of your soil sample in some pure water (either rain water or distilled water). The colour of the paper after dipping it in the solution is then checked against a colour chart that comes with the kit. Green indicates a neutral pH. Yellow through orange to red indicates increasing acidity and blue-green through to deep blue indicates increasing alkalinity.

Checking the pH of your soil is very important as plants will not grow properly if the pH is wrong for them. Some plants, like potatoes, tomatoes, marrows, cucumbers, strawberries, apples, pears and raspberries, enjoy a slightly acid soil (pH 5.5–6.5). Others, such as cabbages and Brussels sprouts, prefer an alkaline soil (pH 7.3–8.0). Lime makes soils alkaline, but too much of it is generally a bad thing because it causes the trace elements, boron and manganese, to be "locked up" and unavailable to plants. This will show up as a deficiency in the plant.

And, if all else fails, and you're not sure what is going on, mulching or digging in compost made from a selection of materials (the more the merrier) will supply all the nutrients you need. You can also add a handful of poultry manure per square metre for good measure.

Plant nutrient	Chemical symbol	How plants look when nutrient is left out of its earthly menu	How you can remedy the situation in your soil
Nitrogen	N	• Pale green or yellow leaves • Poor growth • Stems may be yellow and rigid • Older leaves drop off • Pest problems	Add: • Plenty of organic matter, including compost and manure • Liquid manure/teas • Green manures • Comfrey • Plant legumes • Dried blood, hoof 'n horn, bone meal
Phosphorus (Most of our soils lack phosphorus)	P	• Stunted growth • Purplish leaves • Side shoots and flowers may not form well	Add: • Bones • Bird manures • Rock phosphate • Organic matter, compost and manure
Potassium (A shortage is not common in soils unless they are acidic)	K	• Stems do not elongate as they should, giving plants a compact, dwarfed appearance • Noticeable yellow mottling of leaves, eventually leading to dead areas • Fruits are small and thin-skinned	Add: • Wood ash • Bone meal • Well-composted manures • Seaweed
Calcium	Ca	• Stunted plants with yellow leaves and stunted root growth • Leaves near the growing points may turn brown at the edges and die back • Young leaves may show a purplish-brown tint, while older leaves remain green • Deformed leaves	• Agricultural lime or dolomite added in autumn, both of which contain calcium and magnesium
Magnesium	Mg	• Reduces crop yield • Yellowing of leaves with major veins remaining green (although not as distinct as is common with iron deficiency) • Older leaves are affected first and turn yellow (chlorosis)	• Agricultural lime or dolomite added in winter

We are co-creators of a new world and it all starts in the soil.

Plant nutrient	Chemical symbol	How plants look when nutrient is left out of its earthly menu	How you can remedy the situation in your soil
Boron	B	• Small leaves • Young leaves have dead tissue • Growing points die back • Stems become stiff and straight – if a teaspoon of borax washed into the soil at the base of the plant sorts this out, it's sure to be a boron deficiency	• These micro-nutrients or trace elements are required in tiny amounts so take care not to damage your plants by overdoing any of them – the most satisfactory method of ensuring that they are in your soil is to add seaweed, seaweed concentrates or other marine products to your compost heap • Mulch or a compost of mixed materials supplies all nutrients, plus a cup or so of poultry manure per square metre • A general lack of micro-nutrients causes leaves to die back from the tip
Chlorine	Cl	• Chlorosis (yellowing) of leaves	
Copper	Cu	• Leaves and stems are spindly, grow poorly, with leaves turning yellow and curling upwards • Young growth withers near the tip	
Iron	Fe	• Leaves are pale yellow, almost white in severe cases. • The veins often remain green and distinct (as opposed to other deficiencies where the veins are green but more or less mottled or diffused)	
Manganese	Mn	• Dead spots on the leaves	
Molybdenum	Mo	• Distorted stems • Curling and mottling of older leaves	
Sulphur	S	• Overall pale yellow colour – sulphur works hand-in-hand with nitrogen in making the material for building plant cells • Deficiency symptoms are similar to those of nitrogen	
Zinc	Zn	• Yellowing of tips and edges of leaves as well as deformed leaves • Leaves often narrow and pointed	

In the chapters that follow we will look at some of the ways you can not only feed your soil and plants, but also feed and occupy yourself in ways that are inspiring and environmentally responsible.

CHAPTER FIVE

Building the soil and preparing your beds

*The soil is a great connector of lives, the source and destination of all.
It is the healer and restorer and resurrector, by which disease passes into health,
age into youth, and death to life. Without proper care for it we can have no
human community, because without proper care for it we can have no life.*

ALAN ROSENBERG AND THOMAS LINDERS

Healthy soil = healthy plants = healthy people

It makes sense to go that extra mile when preparing the soil for your food garden. It is an investment in your future health and well-being.

It goes without saying that building the fertility of your garden soil is as vital as the growing of your own food crops, and that the failure to do the first must ultimately spell the demise of the other. Your prime task as a gardener, and custodian of a small patch of the planet, then becomes one of producing shovelfuls of earth that are black with sticky humus which holds water and nutrients around the soil particles; where hungry plant roots have ease of access to what they need for healthy growth. No matter what type of soil you have been blessed with, it is possible to work it so that it will grow whatever crop you wish to grow, with few exceptions.

There are many ways to create a humus-rich soil: by introducing a variety of un-decomposed organic material directly into the soil (trenching and double digging); by digging in large amounts of compost (home-made preferably); by working the soil from the top by mulching; and by making plants work for us. We'll take a look at a variety of methods for improving soil fertility.

Different ways of preparing the soil for planting

Single digging means that the soil is loosened or turned to the depth of one spade-head (30 cm). This method is a good one if your soil is deep and fertile, is not compacted and you have plenty of water. You can increase the amount of organic matter in the top layers by digging in compost or well-rotted manure.

Most soils are poor and compacted, however, and there is also a shortage of water in southern Africa. You will find it better, therefore, to use one of the following methods for the best results:

- Double digging
- Trenching
- Sheet mulching

Double digging

This is a good method for heavy clay soils where drainage is a problem.

First mark out your bed, then dig out all the soil to a depth of 30 cm (the topsoil) and put it to one side. Using a fork, loosen and turn the soil at the bottom of the bed (the subsoil) to a depth of 30 cm. Then add a 10-cm layer of compost, well-rotted manure or any other organic matter in the bottom of the trench. Cover this with the topsoil and shape the bed.

Taking the topsoil and the subsoil together, you should loosen the soil to a depth of two spade-heads (60 cm).

Trenching

This gives the best results by far, especially in very dry areas, or where there is little water and poor soil. It is hard work at first, but your efforts will be well rewarded with bumper crops. It is particularly good in sandy and loamy soils. This is how you go about it.

Digging your first trench

Before you start, collect about 12 black bags of organic waste or "rubbish", which will provide food for the soil. This is what you can collect:

- Fruit and vegetable waste from your home and the local supermarket
- Pot scrapings
- Egg shells, bones, and feathers

Seaweed is a nutrient-rich addition to a trench bed

- Cardboard and paper, avoiding glossy and highly coloured paper
- Lawn clippings
- Dry leaves
- All garden waste, except grass runners and bluegum leaves
- Manure
- Seaweed
- Wood ash from untreated timber
- Untreated wood shavings

Waste not want not. Use your waste to build your soil, rather than sending it to a landfill site.

These materials are not suitable for adding to your trench.

The Aquatrap – an economical solution to water conservation

Let's look at some other materials that you may produce in and around your home or in your business that you could use in your vegetable garden and that will not break down in Nature. Over 100 000 tons of motor vehicle tyres get dumped in South Africa every year. Industry may use some of these used tyres to make other products, but often they are burnt in the townships to recover the tiny pieces of metal inside the walls of the tyre. These recovered bits of metal are then sold on to scrap merchants, but the fires make a terribly toxic and highly visible black smoke when they are burnt in the open.

What else can you do with tyres? Are there any problems if you use them in the garden? I have scattered some suggestions for using this no-cost resource throughout this book, because I believe that – if we use them carefully – we can ease the burden on landfill sites and our already stressed environment. South African, Mark Algra, introduced the idea of slitting tyres in half along their length and then burying them below the soil to conserve water. He first saw this practice in the desert areas of America, where it was also used to conserve water on golf courses. The side wall of a tyre, a piece of inner tube and some contact adhesive are all that are needed to create a simply ingenious device for preventing water from draining too quickly from the upper layers of the soil and away from plant roots, leaching essential nutrients with it. Mark has encouraged community groups to manufacture the Aquatraps for themselves, and to use them in vegetable gardens on the Cape Flats, where sandy soils do not retain water that easily.

Having marked out the first trench bed …

1 Dig out the topsoil (one spade-head or 30 cm deep) and place it to one side of the bed.

2 Dig out the bottom soil (subsoil), also to one spade-head deep, and put this soil on the opposite side of the bed. Remove all large stones and boulders and any other rubbish that will not break down into soil food.

3 Loosen the soil at the bottom of the trench with a fork and cover with a layer of cardboard and newspaper. You can also use Aquatraps (see box) to slow down the rate at which water drains out of the trench.

4 Put a layer (about 20 cm deep) of coarse rubbish at the bottom of the trench and cover it with a 10-cm layer of subsoil. Water both layers well.

5 Now make alternating layers each of brown waste, dry and green waste and wet organic waste, each layer about 20 cm deep.

6 Sprinkle with manure and water and add another 10-cm layer of subsoil.

7 Continue with these layers, removing any tins, bottles, plastic, synthetic (man-made) materials and rubber, until the trench is full. Water each layer well as you go.

8 Place a half-metre stake in each corner of the trench as a bed marker.

9 Now replace the topsoil that you removed from the trench. Add some topsoil from the paths to the top of the bed as well. The surface of the bed ought to be about 15–25 cm higher than the path when you have finished. The bed will slowly sink as the rubbish rots.

10 Spread one bucket of compost, if you have it, over each square metre of bed. Work it in and level the bed using a rake or a flat piece of wood.

11 Cover the bed with a layer of mulch (a protective blanket for the soil and for the delicate roots of your plants). Dry grass, straw, leaves, even newspaper and cardboard, can be used as a mulch. (See the note on "Mulch" on pages 102–3.)

NB: You do not have to layer the organic materials with the subsoil when you are filling the trench. Simply layer the brown, dry and green, wet materials with manure and fill the trench to the top before adding the subsoil, followed by the topsoil, as in the drawings on this page.

You will find that it is best to leave your bed for about a month before planting. This will allow the natural composting process to start below the soil. If, however, you have already added compost or manure to the top layer, you may plant immediately.

Fill the trench with alternating layers of organic waste and subsoil

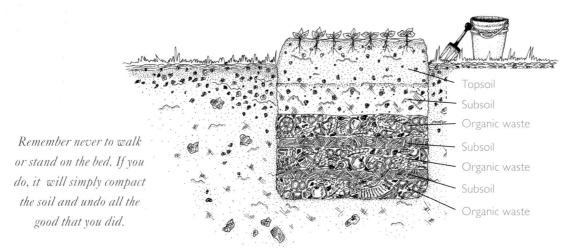

Remember never to walk or stand on the bed. If you do, it will simply compact the soil and undo all the good that you did.

Topsoil
Subsoil
Organic waste
Subsoil
Organic waste
Subsoil
Organic waste

A completed trench bed – a side view

Your waste becomes your health and your wealth ...

Once you have planted the first bed, dig and prepare the second one. You can then plant a month later: this is what we call **succession planting**. Spacing out your plantings at different times is important, because your crops will appear at different times and you can be sure of having something to eat all year round.

Four trench beds, each one about the size of a door, will keep your family with a constant supply of fresh vegetables and herbs. You will be surprised at just how much you can plant in these door-sized beds.

Having prepared the soil and planted your veggie beds for maximum production, your work as a gardener is not complete. Here is the good news: the heavy part is over. As long as you never walk on the beds and keep them covered with compost and mulch, you will never have to work the beds again. You can sit back a little and ponder the wonders of nature while your garden grows.

> A variation on the trenching method is described in the preparation of a circle garden (an "ecocircle") on page 61. If you have access to large amounts of compost (even if it is only partially decomposed), you can layer the subsoil and then the topsoil with compost. See further on.

Trenching is an enormous amount of work in the beginning, but it is undoubtedly the most effective way to boost your soil:

- It increases the soil nutrient and humus levels
- It provides food to support a whole host of soil flora and fauna
- It reverses the damage of compaction (reduced air in the soil and its water-holding capacity)
- The organic matter that you bury in the soil acts as a sponge and holds water, reducing water use and the leaching of nutrients

Soil preparation is the food gardener's most important task. Hard work it may seem but it pays off in the end, with increased production in small spaces and with a major boost to soil fertility and to your health.

And remember: this method is a most efficient, effective and environmentally sound way to recycle household and garden waste.

Sheet mulching or composting

Build your soil the "no work" way

Sheet mulching (or composting) is the simplest method of building the fertility of most soil types. It also demands the least labour and does not need the back-breaking spade work for setting up a new garden.

What's more, mulching encourages the living creatures of the soil. Many of these creatures will work the soil over for you – no digging required. It is a three-in-one method which combines composting, mulching and the destruction of weeds through the use of materials which break down naturally (called **biodegradable materials**, such as cardboard and newspaper).

We will discuss two of the many ways of sheet mulching. Both need masses of organic matter in the beginning. After that, you will become used to adding more mulching materials to the surface after the creatures in the soil have broken down the mulch into life-sustaining humus. The whole idea behind mulching is to disturb the soil as little as possible.

Here's how to go about it...

Method 1

- Mark out the areas for your new beds.
- For acid soils, sprinkle some rock phosphate, or bone meal and wood ash, or dolomitic lime on top of whatever is there, be it bare soil, weeds, grass.
- For acid soils, sprinkle some sulphur on top.

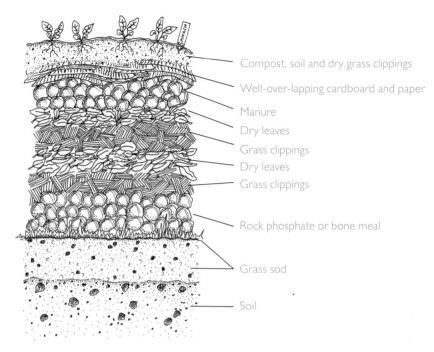

Compost, soil and dry grass clippings

Well-over-lapping cardboard and paper

Manure

Dry leaves

Grass clippings

Dry leaves

Grass clippings

Rock phosphate or bone meal

Grass sod

Soil

Sheet mulch gardening

- Cover the area with a layer of manure. This will provide the extra nitrogen needed to break down those leaves and roots of the plants that will be buried by the mulching materials.
- Add alternating layers (6 cm or three fingers deep) as follows:
  - green, wet materials (lawn clippings, fresh leaves and prunings);
  - brown, dry materials (untreated sawdust, autumn leaves, straw); and
  - more manure
- Water each layer as you go, until you have covered the demarcated area to a depth of at least 20cm.
- With vigorous Kikuyu grass, mulch the area up to 30 or 40 cm deep. You'll be surprised at how much organic matter it takes to do this.
- Cover the whole area with *overlapping* sheets of newspaper (3–5 sheets) or cardboard (1–3 sheets). This will stop the weed seeds from germinating and the grass runners from creeping through. These will otherwise compete with your plants for sunlight, food, air and water.
- Wet the paper and cardboard thoroughly and, in a very short space of time, it will have rotted down and disappeared.
- Lastly, add a layer of compost, soil and mulch to hide the unsightly newspaper and – hey presto! – you're ready to plant.
- Make a hole in the mulch and soil layer.
- Cut a cross through the paper or cardboard.
- Add a bucket of good potting mix (half compost, half good garden soil).
- Sow your seed or transplant your seedlings or plant cuttings.
- Water well.

Method 2

- Mark out the areas for your new beds.
- Cover whatever is there (bare soil, weeds, grass) with 3–6 sheets of newspaper or 1–3 sheets of cardboard.
- Make sure the sheets are overlapping well, and water.
- Now carry on as in Method 1 above, layering green, wet and brown, dry materials and manure until the bed area is covered to a depth of at least 20 cm.
- Add a layer of mulch to cover.
- To plant up this sheet-mulched area, simply make a hole in the mulch, add a good soil mix and plant.

Using both methods, you will not need herbicides or other drastic measures to kill the grass and other vegetation. The newspaper and cardboard will do it for you. A myriad different creatures will take up residence in this bountiful environment, enriching the soil beneath with valuable humus, which will be worked in by earthworms and other organisms. In effect, they will dig the soil for you.

Make your own compost …

It's easy to make and easy to use. There are many ways to turn valuable household, garden and agricultural waste into sweet-smelling, moist, black, velvety, humus-rich compost. If you make a compost heap (see the instructions in Chapter 8, it will give you a source of your own valuable humus, the quality of which far outstrips what you can buy from local outlets).

Work with earthworms …

Worm manure (also known as "castings") is rich in microbial life, minerals and micro-nutrients. It increases the humus content of the soil and provides food for other beneficial micro-organisms, which in turn continue the composting and humus-building process. For more on these wonder workers, go to Chapter 6.

Mulch, mulch and mulch some more …

This is the single most important task for any gardener. Cover your soil with whatever organic material you can find. Any dry material – wood chips, dry grass and leaves, pine needles, corn cobs, paper, cardboard – will act as a barrier to retain moisture, insulate and stabilise the soil, protect plants and control weeds. They will also be broken down by soil organisms into soil food, thereby feeding and building the soil from the top down. Mulch also provides a place to live for garden predators and other useful creatures.

And here are some more tips …

- Soil-building can also be achieved by working with your plants. Grow lots of legumes and dig in their remains once you have harvested the produce. Rotate the light-feeding root crops – for example, carrots, radishes, turnips, beetroot and parsnips with heavy feeders – leaf and fruit crops – for example, cabbage, spinach, lettuce, tomatoes, pumpkins and squash, green peppers, brinjals and legumes.
- Interplant your beds with a wide range of plants that support each other and the soil.
- Never be tempted to use agro-chemicals (artificial fertilisers and synthetic pesticides).
- Plant green manure crops like lucerne and dig them in when the stems are about 10 cm high.
- Plant ground covers like New Zealand spinach, chou (sou sou) marrows, and the cucurbit family to protect the soil from the heat of the sun, from wind, from heavy rain and hail, which compact the soil and cause capping,

Mulch, mulch, mulch: the single most important task for any gardener

a thin surface layer of the soil becomes compacted and this makes it difficult for tiny seedlings to break through to reach the sunlight.

• Dig the soil as little as possible. The less you dig, the less disturbance there is to the soil life.

Preparing the beds

You have already designed the layout for your food garden, having decided if you were going to incorporate it into your existing garden, or whether it was going to be integrated into the bigger picture. It may not have been important to you to create a masterpiece of design, because vegetables and fruit trees are decorative in their own way. Even the most regimented beds with everything growing in straight rows can look eye-catching. What you planned for was not only visual appeal, but also convenience and high yields.

Rectangular plots are perhaps the most practical, never more than a metre wide (so that you never trample the well-prepared soil) and as long as your garden will allow. Pathways between beds should be minimised – unproductive space – and never more than about ½ metre wide. You can build your beds within the allotted space with these principles in mind and a whole gamut of creativity. Paths can serve a double function; as walkways, and as composting sites. Covered with newspaper or cardboard to restrict weed growth, and in turn covered with mulch, the soil beneath will be converted into a beautiful loam while you work. When you need to raise the beds, the composted soil you need is ready and waiting on the paths.

Curved beds have their place and create a softness. Half-moons and horseshoes, concentric circles, and pizza-slice beds could all have their part in your food garden. The same principles apply.

With the digging done, all that remains is to make the actual bed. It is a good idea, particular if you have heavy clay soils that do not drain well, to raise the bed level about 15 to 20 cm above the surrounding ground. This improves drainage, increases the rooting depth, allows soil to warm up quickly in spring and improves aeration. Bed edges may be built up with bricks, wood or whatever you have available.

In very dry areas of the country, rather make sunken beds that will capture any rain and sink it deep into the soil before it runs off, carrying precious topsoil with it. The sides of such beds act as shelters from the wind for seedlings and prevent seeds being blown away.

"Ecocircles" or circle gardens - a discovery *par excellence*

Circles of cultivation

Save water and increase production with a new way of gardening
I first read about "ecocircles" ("circles of cultivation") in a *Land* magazine dating back to 1998. The article was written by Anthony Trowbridge of Applied Natural Sciences at the Technikon SA. In a telephone conversation with him, he enthusiastically endorsed this way of growing as a means not only to save on labour, but also to provide a unique and simple way of growing large amounts of food in small spaces using very little water. Not only can the method be effectively used by the home gardener, but it can also be used on a commercial scale, where its low-tech requirements reduce capital costs.

Professor Donald Langham, working in Venezuela, developed the idea of planting in circles instead of growing in straight lines in angular beds as a means of overcoming the difficulties faced by South American farmers; the same difficulties experienced in this country with an ever-increasing prospect of drought and, in some regions, floods and the loss of precious topsoil.

It affords the home gardener an opportunity to create interesting garden designs with circular veggie patches arranged along pathways, interspersed with herbs and flowers. These serve multiple purposes by attracting beneficial animal life, providing colour and diversity, acting as companion plants to the vegetable crops, stimulating their growth, acting as natural pest deterrents and creating a feeling of abundance.

There are many benefits of growing in this way:

- You can grow lots of food in small spaces. Each circle has a diameter of one metre (or one spade). You will be surprised at how much food you can harvest from one of these circles. Raised beds give an increased depth for establishing healthy root systems.

- There is a saving of up to 70% in water usage. Compost (or other organic material) added to the soil as the bed is constructed, creates a sponge which retains the water. Mulching prevents evaporation and the method of irrigating ensures that minimum water is used.

- "Ecocircles" build soil fertility and help to prevent the unnecessary loss of soil to the erosive forces of wind and rain.

- The basin shape of the completed bed funnels water into the centre where it sinks into the soil; it doesn't run off, carrying precious topsoil with it. In other words, the bed acts as a mini water-harvester.

- Deep watering encourages good root growth. A strong, well-developed root system will ensure a healthy plant.

- Because it is such simple technology, it costs nothing to implement. Very important in this day and age of prohibitive costs.

- It requires almost nil land preparation. You don't even need to weed before you start. This means less work for those of us who are not up to wielding a spade.

If you're ready to give it a go – this is how you go about creating your first ecocircle:

1. Mark out a circle (one metre in diameter) on the ground using two sticks and a piece of string. Alternatively, if you are the secret possessor of a hoola hoop, that will suffice to mark out the circle.

2. Remove the first 20–30 cm of topsoil and place in a neat pile next to the circle.

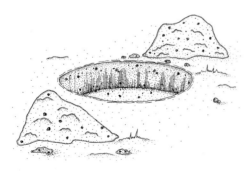

3. Remove 20–30 cm of subsoil and place it in a separate pile next to the circle. The depth of the hole should be 50 cm (knee deep).

4. Using a candle and a needle (stick it in a cork to prevent burning your fingers), burn 16 holes in the side of a 2-litre plastic bottle which has a lid. The holes should be arranged at four different levels.

5. Place the bottle at the bottom of the hole, in the centre of the circle. Add a 2-cm layer (one finger) of compost (or well-rotted kraal manure, kitchen waste or dry grass) in the base of the hole and cover this with an 8-cm layer (four fingers) of subsoil. Water these two layers well.

6. Continue replacing the subsoil, layering it with compost (or the other materials mentioned above) and watering each layer as you go until all the subsoil has been replaced.

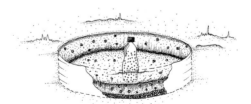

By adding organic matter and watering each level in turn, a sponge effect is created which will retain water below the surface so that plant roots are encouraged to grow downwards, giving them greater strength. Surface watering tends to make plant roots stay near the surface.

The sponge effect is maintained by the burying of the bottle (or alternatively a tin can with holes in the bottom) into which water can be poured so that all the plants in the ecocircle can be reached with one watering session.

Having added all the subsoil, replace the topsoil. The surface of the bed will be higher than the surrounding ground. This creates a raised circular bed.

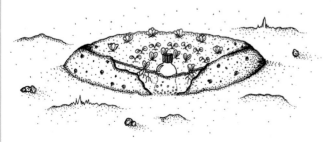

Scoop the soil from the centre of the circle to the outside to create a basin with the top of the bottle in the centre.

Mulch the surface of the basin and plant seeds or seedlings on the inside of the ridge, in circles. It is extremely important to keep the beds well mulched as this prevents water loss by evaporation.

One bed can accommodate 10 lettuces, 5 to 8 cabbages or 4 rows of beans or a variety of different crops.

To look after your "ecocircle" there are
a few things you need to remember:

- Fill the bottle with water. It is only necessary to do this once a week, if the bed is well mulched. This means that you are using only 2 litres of water per bed per week. Tighten the cap and then loosen a little so that no vacuum is created once the water drips out into the soil.
- In areas of high rainfall, the surface of the bed should be flat to prevent water-logging. In dry areas, the basin shape promotes the sinking of water.
- Records on planting and crop rotation can be kept easily and accurately to ensure good soil and, therefore, good plant health.
- Very young seedlings planted in the centre of the circle are protected from wind.

CHAPTER SIX

Earthworms: your best partners in the garden

Earthworms bring amazing benefits to your garden …

- They aerate the soil by their burrowing – sometimes as far as two metres deep.
- Their tunnels make passages for water to penetrate deeply into the soil.
- They improve the ability of the soil to retain water by pulverising soil and creating tunnels in their search for food. You can see earthworm tunnels when you turn over dry soil.
- They create topsoil and maintain soil fertility. By ingesting the soil, they loosen it and bring the deeper parts of the soil (often rich in minerals) to the surface.
- They hasten the breakdown of organic waste and turn it into humus. It has been estimated that in a half-hectare of healthy soil, there may be as many as one million earthworms and these can produce about one ton of humus fertiliser every 24 hours.
- They incorporate organic waste into the soil in the form of rich castings which are immediately available for use by plants. These castings are far richer in minerals than the soil.
- They reduce the need for artificial fertilisers, which are not only expensive, but also damage the soil structure and organisms.
- They are able to transform tons of organic waste into rich compost (vermi-compost) to use in and on the soil.
- They are wonderful converters of waste fruit from orchards and help to prevent the spread of fungal diseases.
- They produce enzymes, hormones, vitamins and antibiotics, thereby increasing the immunity of plants against pests and diseases.

Facts about earthworms

• Because earthworms have no skin pigments to protect them, even a little sunlight can kill them., which is why they have to be kept in the dark.

• Earthworms move by using a system of hydraulics and small bristles (chaetae or setae) on the sides of their bodies. If you put a worm on a piece of paper, and listen very carefully, you will be able to hear a soft scratching noise.

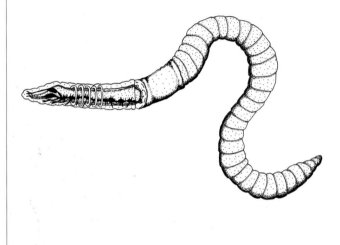

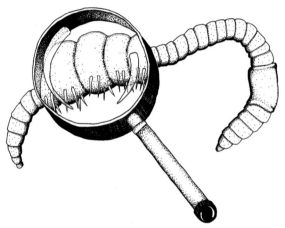

• Earthworms have five pairs of hearts. If you use a magnifying glass, you will see a pulsating red blood vessel which runs along its back.
• Human beings and earthworms have the same blood pigment – haemoglobin.
• Because they breathe through their skins, they thrive in moist soil. Make sure that your compost heap or garden soil is always damp.
• Their bodies are covered in mucus, which helps to keep them moist. They also use their mucus to package their own waste.

Learning about earthworms is absolutely fascinating. What you learnt at school was interesting enough, but you didn't get even a smidgen of information. Make an effort to read more about them. If you have a thorough understanding of the life-cycle of the earthworm, you will know exactly what is going on in your "farm".

If you want to produce humus for your garden soil, you may find that you do not have the space or enough organic waste to set up compost heaps. Don't despair, because the "recycling wonders" of the world will do it for you in a very small space, even in a box outside your kitchen door. Earthworms are your solution to disposing of waste, and providing you with a cost-free source of high-quality fertiliser. As somebody once said, they work around the clock, do not demand a wage and never go on strike. All you have to do is provide them with a supply of food and make sure that they are kept cool, moist and in the dark, literally.

Some common earthworms

The planet has over 3 000 varieties of earthworms. They come in all sizes and hues of red, brown and silvery grey and they can tackle vast quantities of decaying plant and animal remains: from whole chicken carcasses to your kitchen scrapings and peelings. You will find a worm variety for everything.

Most types of earthworms do not like to be kept in containers and many do not breed fast enough to make a significant impact on your waste. Only four types of earthworms are used for "farming" in general:

1 Night crawlers

Description: About 12–15 cm long, light grey to silver in colour, thick and solid-looking.

When you bring them to the surface, night crawlers wriggle vigorously in an attempt to get away from the damaging sunlight. You often see them on lawns after heavy rains when they escape from water-logged burrows. You may also recognise the small heaps of castings they leave at the surface after a night out and about. Because of their deep burrowing habits, they will not work for your worm farm.

2 Red worms (sometimes called "Red wigglers")

Description: About 6-10 cm long, red on top and sometimes paler and flatter underneath.

You will find these worms in gardens and lawns, moist, rotting compost heaps and among leaf mould. You will also find them underneath pot-plant containers where it is dark and moist. They do well wherever there is moist, organic material or soil covered with mulch.

3 Manure worms (also called "Red wigglers")

Description: Similar to the red worm but do not have the flat, pale underside. They have fairly obvious rings around their bodies, giving them a stripy appearance, so they are sometimes called "tiger worms". Their scientific name is *Eisenia fetida*.

Red worms and manure worms are very often found together in earthworm farms, as they both do the same excellent job of vermi-composting or producing castings. These are the worms you must get hold of to set up your earthworm bin.

More wonders of the lowly earthworm

Earthworms can increase the capacity of the soil to hold water up to 350%. This works to help the plants resist drought.

Vermi-compost...

- stops plant nutrients from being leached from the top layers of the soil where they are accessible to roots.
- helps to protect plants against attack by disease organisms, such as viruses, bacteria and fungi.
- contains
  - five times more nitrogen
  - eleven times more potassium
  - three times more magnesium and
  - twice as much calcium as the soil the earthworms ingested along with their food.

How to prepare for your earthworm farm

An earthworm farm or worm bin is nothing more than a compost heap that is contained.

The container must help to:

- conserve moisture
- provide darkness for the worms, and
- maintain a more or less constant temperature.

You will also need:

- some worms to get started
- waste material for them to eat (vegetable waste from the kitchen is ideal)
- some manure for added nitrogen, and
- some rougher bedding material like dry leaves, straw or paper.

How to choose your container

You can "farm" worms in almost anything: from old baths and "44-gallon" drums to polystyrene ice boxes, buckets and old fridges. Wooden boxes are ideal because wood is a good insulator and it also breathes. Plastic, on the other hand, is a poor insulator and does not breathe at all. You will have to punch holes in the sides and bottom to let the air in and out.

Select a container that you have used before for something else. This not only reduces your starting costs, but keeps to the spirit of recycling – the true essence of the humble earthworm. Through this and other daily methods of recycling, you will help to slow down the demand on the world's finite and fast-dwindling resources.

The ideal bin should have a large surface area and be about 30 to 40 cm in depth.

Old baths make ideal worm farms

How to set up your earthworm farm

- Place the worm bin in a shaded and sheltered position. Worms do not like to be hot, so make sure that, wherever you put them, the temperature remains between 13°C and 27°C. Choose a quiet place because earthworms do not like loud noises.
- Set your container up on some legs so that the liquid (liquid manure or "worm tea") can drain out and be collected. You may also want to stand the legs in cans of water to stop ants and other predators from attacking the worms. Smearing a band of grease around the legs also acts as a deterrent.
- Cover the bottom of the bin with hessian (sack cloth), plastic mesh bags or some other liner that will stop the worms from escaping through the holes. You will also need to make sure that the worm castings stay in the container.
- Prepare your bedding material, which is any loose, organic material that retains water. For example:
  - leaf mould
  - dry leaves mixed with shredded newspaper
  - straw
  - shredded cardboard
  - grass clippings
- Make sure the bedding material is moist before you put it into the bin. First soak it in a bucket of water and then wring it out so that it is as moist as a damp sponge. Soak shredded paper overnight in water to remove any damaging chemicals, particularly chlorine, which is normally used to bleach the paper white.
- Add a layer of bedding, 5–10 cm deep.
- Fill the bin with well-rotted animal manure or vegetable waste which has been chopped into small pieces.

A handful of "lowly" earthworms

- Add the worms and cover them and their food with a layer of damp mulch, which can be a mixture of dry grass, leaves, moss, old cloths, hessian bags, newspaper or straw.
- Put a lid on the bin so that the worms cannot be eaten by garden birds.

How many worms will your kitchen waste feed?

If you want to add all your waste to your earthworm bin every day, you will have to do some sums. Too much food and too few worms spell disaster for the worm bin.

STEP ONE

Work out what one worm eats in a day. Each worm will eat about half its body weight in food daily. An average adult red wriggler weighs about one gram. So one worm will eat half a gram of waste a day. Remember to take into account that you will have worms of all different agaes and sizes in your bin.

STEP TWO

Work out what how much waste you produce in your kitchen in a day.

- Put an ice-cream tub next to the sink and put all your peelings, scraps and whatever else in that. At the end of the day, weigh it. Do this for a week and work out your average daily waste production (the mass of the waste divided by seven days).
- Multiply your average daily figure by two and that will give you the number of worms that your household needs.
- Don't forget that the population will build up if the worms are happy. So you can –
  - process more waste
  - give worms to your friends and family
  - put them in your garden (if it is very well mulched), or
  - add them to a cold compost heap.

Feeding the worms

Don't give them too much food all at the same time. Put small amounts underneath the covering and wait until they have nearly completed what you gave them last. Chop the food into small pieces so that they can deal with it faster. Earthworms do not have teeth.

Don't think you can get away with giving them the same old things day after day. The same principle of a restricted diet applies to earthworms.

The process of decomposition may be slow in the beginning because the worms usually take about six weeks to build up their population. Breeding worms on a diet of waste is slower than feeding them on manure.

Collect the liquid manure (worm tea), which drains through the holes in the bottom of the worm bin. Use it to fertilise your plants and to build the soil. Not only is it full of nutrients, but it also contains microbes, which add life to the soil.

Worm tea is a liquid manure

OPTION ONE
Use the liquid that drains through the holes at the bottom of
your bin.

OPTION TWO
Tie a big handful of vermi-compost in an old stocking or piece
of net curtain and leave it to soak in 2 litres of water for a day
or two.
Not only is it full of a range of nutrients, but it is teeming with
miniature life (microbes) that will boost your soil population. It
is better to use fresh worm tea, but if you put it in a sealed glass
bottle, it will keep for a few months.

What to feed your earthworms

Vegetables (including peels and tops), fruit (peels and
flesh), coffee grounds (including the filter), tea leaves and
tea bags, bread, rice, mealie meal, pasta, cakes, muffins,
biscuits, lunch-box leftovers, pot scrapings, old flower
arrangements, crushed egg-shells, paper, egg boxes and
wine sleeves.

You can also add the following, depending on the size
of your worm bin: garden waste, partially decomposed
compost, and well-rotted manure from horses, cows,
donkeys and chickens. Actually, you can use the manure
from any plant-eating animals, but it must be "old"
manure, because fresh droppings will heat up when they
are added to the bin and will "cook" the worms.

Leave out the following foods and materials

Citrus fruits, meat and bones, garlic, heavily spiced foods,
hair, dairy products, fresh green wastes and manure, fats
and oils, salt, wood ashes, pets' faeces, and household
and garden chemicals.

How much food can a worm eat?

Worms can eat up to half their body weight in food per
day when conditions are just right for them. There are
approximately 2 000 worms per kg. Generally speaking,
one kilogram of earthworms will eat half a kilogram of
organic material per day. Under perfect conditions, this
could go up to one kilogram of organic waste per day, but
under poor conditions the amount will fall to less than half
a kilogram in 24 hours. If you watch carefully the amount
of food that is eaten by the worms, you will soon know how
well your worms are doing.

*Remember that this is an artificial environment.
The worms cannot move away when things
get uncomfortable. Keep an eye on
conditions in your worm bin …*

How many worms will it take to fill your bin?

The easiest way to calculate this is to work out roughly the
surface area of the top of your bin. For every 400 cm² of surface
in your worm bin, you will need about 100 adult worms, each
weighing about 1 g; or about nine worms per tea-bag surface.

STEP ONE
Cut out a template from a piece of paper or card – 20 cm by 20
cm. The surface area of this template is 400 cm² – about nine
square tea bags (an easier way of measuring, if your bin is small).

STEP TWO
Put your template on top of the bin. See how many times it
fits side by side until all the area is used up. So, if the surface
of your bin measures 2 500 cm², about 700 worms will make a
good start. That's about ¾ kg of worms! This weight will include
the worm compost that comes with the worms when you buy
them. And don't forget: this is only your start-up number. If
they're happy, the population will grow fairly rapidly.

Temperature

Keep the worm bedding at temperatures between 15° and 25° C. The best temperature is around 24°–25° C.

• In very cold areas in winter, move the bin indoors. Otherwise, you can insulate the bin by wrapping cardboard or an old blanket around it.

• In summer, high temperatures can kill the worms. Check the position of your bin. Make sure that it is located in a shady, well-ventilated spot.

• When the surrounding temperature goes up at midday in high summer, you may want to move the bin to a cooler part of your house or garden. Add extra bedding and keep air flowing through the system. The moisture in the bedding will evaporate with good airflow and keep the worms cooler. Make sure that the bedding is kept moist enough for this to happen.

Moisture levels

These should be kept between 75% and 90% (damp but not soggy).

• In dry conditions keep the bin covered. A moisture meter is useful if you are unsure of how damp to keep the bin.

pH levels

(a measure of acidity or alkalinity)

• The pH of the bin should be 7 (neutral). A pH meter is a useful instrument if you are unsure.

Aeration

(the flow of air in and out of the bin)

• Oxygen levels must be kept high for two reasons.

  1 The aerobic (oxygen-loving) bacteria need oxygen to keep them happy, so that they can break down the organic material to feed the worms.

  2 Oxygen is necessary for the survival of the worms.

All is not well if the bin starts to smell …

If you want to have good aeration, keep the bedding loose and make sure that the bin has plenty of air and drainage holes. You may even need to turn the bedding once in a while to make sure that enough air gets into the bin.

How to harvest a worm bin

• When a worm bin is full, scoop out any undigested food scraps and the material that contains the most worms (usually the top 10–12 cm of material).

• Use the rest as compost.

• Put the material that is full of worms back into the bin.

• Mix it with an equal amount of bedding, and cover with 2–3 cm of shredded paper.

• If you want to remove more worms from the compost, spread a thin layer on a piece of canvas in the sunlight, leaving a few small mounds. The worms will gather in the mounds as the material dries. Be careful, though, because the heat and rapid drying can kill the worms.

• Another method you can try is to sift the compost gently over a wire screen and save the worms that don't go through. The resulting humus-rich soil, after cleaning out the worms, can be used for nursery soil. Mix three parts river sand to one part humus. You can also use this mixture as a top dressing around your plants.

After the worm bin has been going for a few months, animals other than earthworms often appear. These may include mites, ants, beetles, centipedes, snails and other members of the compost community. They are part of a normal, balanced environment and cause no harm whatsoever. In fact, if you add compost as a bedding material to your worm bin, you will probably find more kinds of organisms than if you used only newspaper as bedding.

Left: An earthworm farm made out of a recycled tyre

Inside an earthworm farm

It may be doubted whether there are many animals which have played so important a part in the history of the world as have these lowly organised creatures.

Calling earthworms to your garden soil naturally

If you do not want the hassle of developing your own worm-composting bin, you can always attract earthworms to your garden by:

- mulching heavily and keeping the soil damp
- leaving grass clippings on your lawn when you mow
- adding worms to your compost heap
- using natural fertilisers and never resorting to man-made or synthetic agro-chemicals
- never over-tilling your soil
- adding garden lime to acid soils

There is not much point in adding earthworms to your garden soil unless it contains lots of organic matter, is moist and well mulched.

How to use vermi-compost (castings) and worm tea in your garden

Vermi-compost (castings) is used in much smaller amounts than ordinary compost:

- Add it directly to your soil.
- Place it in the hole you have dug before you transplant your seedlings – about one teaspoon per seedling.
- Use it as a top dressing around established plants. About one to two cups of vermi-compost per tree will give a significant boost to growth. Sprinkle the castings onto the soil around the base of the plant to the edge of its canopy. This is where the feeder roots will benefit most from it.
- Add to the soil mix for container plants at the rate of one part of castings to three parts of potting soil. You can also fork it lightly and quite often into the surface of the soil.

- Use it to make a seedling mix for your nursery. Mix sifted potting soil, compost, river sand and castings. A little vermiculite added to this mixture will help to retain water.

Use the worm tea to water:

- container plants (dilute the tea with an equal part of water before using it);
- plants that are in the ground (full strength);
- the leaves of plants (diluted and sprayed gently);
- your lawn (water the lawn well first; sprinkle the vermi-compost evenly over the lawn; water well again).

Worm tea revitalises potting soil; it is especially good for weak or diseased plants; and the roots of stressed plants grow more vigorously after using it.

Perhaps we can tell you a really important reason why we want to encourage enormous populations of these incredible creatures in your garden. Earthworms can help with the alarming problem of greenhouse gases and global warming.

We consume far too many resources, as though our very lives depend on it. We also produce masses of waste products, which are being dumped in bigger and bigger landfill sites.

In his book *Organic Growing with Worms*, David Murphy shows how worms can lock up the carbon dioxide that we are pouring into the atmosphere. He says that in these dump-sites, organic wastes from our cities cannot be broken down by useful life forms. The waste is deliberately covered in bags of plastic film, without benefit of oxygen, and so adds to the destruction of our planet.

Over time, 50 per cent of the carbon (the most prolific element in life forms) buried with organic waste in landfill tips is converted to methane gas. The gas percolates up through the top of the dump and into the atmosphere, where it adds its share to global warming. Yet that very same carbon ought to be used to bring life to our agricultural soil. "In soil, carbon creates life. In landfill tips, it creates poison." Professor Alessandro Piccolo teaches at the University of Naples in Italy. He says that annually we are generating around 15 to 18 billion tonnes of carbon dioxide. The level of organic matter in our soil used to be 20 per cent and now averages less than one percent.

Yet, according to Professor Piccolo, if we were to increase the levels of organic matter in our soil by five percent to a depth of 25 cm, we would lock away 150 billion tonnes of carbon dioxide in the soil.

It is madness to keep on burying organic waste in plastic bags underground in landfill sites when we have so many willing (and able) worms to do the job for free.

Charles Darwin's classic study of earthworms, *The formation of vegetable mould through the action of earthworms, with observations of their habits*, was published in 1881, shortly before his death. Since that time, the importance of worms has been increasingly recognised. The following quotation from Darwin's book is worth thinking about by anybody who has their hands in the soil:

"It may be doubted whether there are many other animals which have played so important a part in the history of the world as have these lowly organised creatures."

Right now, round the world, the demand for these "tillers of the soil" is beginning to exceed supply. They may well be our saviours.

CHAPTER SEVEN

Planting out your garden

Things to think about before you start planting

- Plant what you will eat.
- Use fresh seed. Old seed will not germinate and you will have wasted time.
- Practise inter-planting (or mixed cropping) and crop rotation.
- Plant in the correct season for a healthy crop (see the planting guide on pages 174–6).

Measure with your hand

Add this useful measuring device to your gardening tool box…

20 cm – from the tip of your pinkie finger to the tip of your thumb. Just the right distance for planting seeds and seedlings in the rows.

10 cm – the length of the index finger, from the tip to the knuckle. A good measure for seedlings that are ready to be transplanted. It's also the width across your fingers.

20 cm + 10 cm – the distance between rows when you're planting kale.

3 x 1 cm between seeds gives radishes enough space to swell out into crisp red roots. This will add a hot crunch to your summer salad.

Variety is the spice of life

The greater the variety of plants that you plant:

- the bigger the chances of a successful harvest;
- the better for your health; and
- the better for the health of the soil.

Choose among the following four different kinds of vegetable crops and grow a rich variety in each and every bed.

Leaf crops

Spinach, Swiss Chard spinach, New Zealand spinach, lettuce, parsley, and the crucifer family – cabbage, cauliflower, kale, broccoli, kohlrabi and Brussels sprouts.

Leaf crops are generally cool-season crops and many can tolerate partial shade. They have a fairly shallow root system, which is shaped like half a ball. These plants are very heavy feeders and take a lot of nutrients out of the soil. Before you start your planting, add well-rotted manure and compost to the soil.

Fruit crops

Tomatoes, egg-plant (aubergine or brinjal), peppers, chillies, pumpkin, squash, marrow, melon, sweet-corn, mealies and cucumber.

These all develop from the flower of the plant. They are warm-season crops and like full sun if they are to do well. Potatoes are also included here, although they are actually swollen underground stems (tubers). Fruit crops do not require as much feeding as the leaf crops, but they also benefit from the addition of compost or manure to the soil before planting. If the tomatoes and potatoes show a good canopy of leaves, then you will have a rich harvest.

Root crops

Carrots, turnips, beetroots and parsnips.
Onions, leeks, shallots and chives are also included in this category although what you're used to eating is not a root, but a collection of swollen leaf bases. They are light feeders with small, shallow root systems. *Never* add manure or compost to the soil before planting, as they may develop forked, hairy roots and too much top growth at the expense of the roots.

Legumes

Peas, beans, broad beans and lucerne (alfalfa), chick peas, lentils, cow and pigeon peas.

This group is very good for you, because they are a fine source of protein. They are also great for soil health because they build up the soil's contents (more about this later). Always make sure to dig their remains back into the soil after the edible part of the crop has been harvested.

The information on "companion planting" later on in this chapter will also help you to decide on how to plant your bed for maximum yield. Plants are very like us humans in that they too have likes and dislikes which you must keep in mind if you want their co-operation and a bumper harvest.

With a little thought and careful planning, you will be able to plant nine to ten rows of vegetables in a bed that is two metres long, making full use of all the space. The diagram on the opposite page gives you an idea of how a bed could be planted.

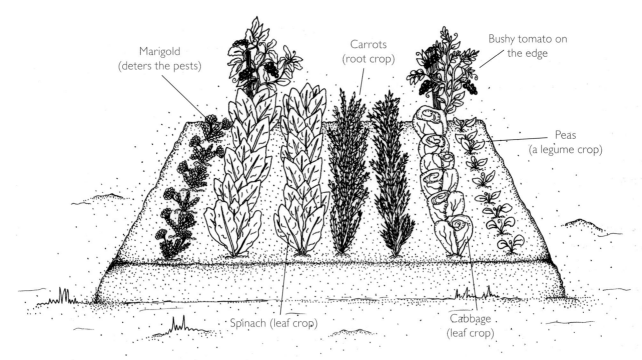

Marigold
(deters the pests)

Carrots
(root crop)

Bushy tomato on
the edge

Peas
(a legume crop)

Spinach (leaf crop)

Cabbage
(leaf crop)

A typical door-size bed fully planted with a variety of crops. This is what is known as "inter-planting" or "mixed cropping".

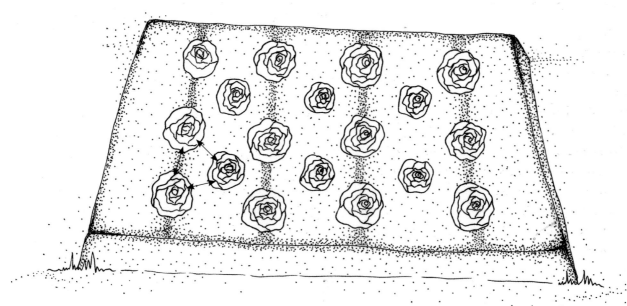

Staggered spacing means that planting space is used productively

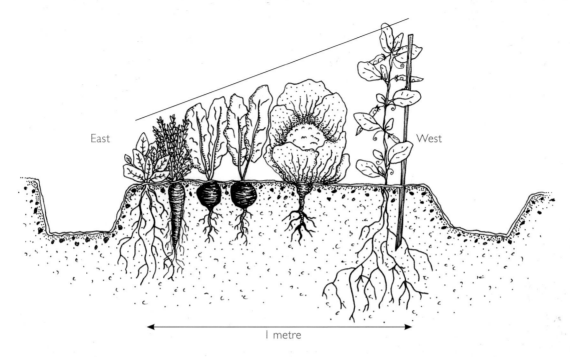

East

West

1 metre

Getting back to the roots again

If you look at the drawing above of a typical bed, you will notice that roots differ in length and feed at different depths.

Notice …

- the variety of vegetables in the bed;
- the different heights of the plants and the lengths of the roots;
- some vegetables have big leaves and need room to spread, others are small;
- some are tall, others are short;
- some like a bit of shade, others like full sun;
- the taller plants are on the west side of the bed. They will protect shade-loving plants from the scorching heat of the afternoon sun. Note also that no shade falls on the plants in the morning.

- The surface of the bed is completely covered with mulch, as are the paths.

"Staggered spacing" means to plant out seedlings at equal distances from each other. This is the best spacing pattern, particularly for large plants such as cabbages, tomatoes and broad beans. Every plant is the same distance from its neighbours in all directions and no space is lost by the gap between the rows.

Look up the growth habits of the different plants before you start sowing seed. Make sure that you do not overcrowd the plants, or waste space by planting them too far apart. Make use of every little bit of space in a bed. You worked hard to make the bed, so you will want a big harvest in return.

Never be tempted to plant only one type of vegetable in a bed!

All you need is your planting guide, a list of vegetables that you want to plant and a bit of creativity. Then you can harvest not only a lot of different vegetables, but also large amounts of them from a very small space. This is because the soil has been so well prepared that is contains a large store of organic matter in it. The vegetables do not have to compete with each other for the nutrients they need. Also, because the soil is so loose, the roots of the plants can penetrate deep in order to seek out the essential minerals.

Now let's get down to business…

How to sow your seed

- Sow the seeds directly into the vegetable bed by parting the mulch and making furrows or grooves which run across the length of the bed. The distance between the rows will vary according to the crop. Use your hand as a rough guide for planting distances.
- Starting at one end of the bed, plant at least three (and, if possible, up to five) different vegetables in each bed in alternating rows; one or two rows from each of the different groups mentioned above.
- Plant in lines that run across the length of the bed. Nature may not grow things in straight lines, but, for the novice, they make it easier to detect the weeds that are bound to pop up out of newly dug soil. Also, straight lines make harvesting easier if you have the same plants together, rather than scattered all over the veggie patch.
- Sow directly into the garden bed if possible, because this will reduce the shock of transplanting seedlings.
- Use your finger to make little grooves in straight lines in the soil for smaller seeds; use the dibber to make holes for larger seeds. Remember the "rule of thumb" for planting depth.

- Place the seed into the grooves, always sowing a few more than you need, in case some don't germinate. But try not to waste seed either by over-planting.
- Cover the seeds with soil from either side of the grooves.
- Press down with the side of your hand so that they are in close contact with the soil.
- Water them gently with a watering can.
- If the weather is very hot and dry, cover the areas where you planted the seeds with a very fine layer of mulch – so thin that you can still see the soil through it.
- Check every day, twice a day, to make sure that the seeds do not dry out.
- Remove the mulch covering the seedlings as soon as they come through the soil so that they are not deprived of sunlight.

To speed up germination

Before planting large seeds – such as beans, peas, mealies, spinach, beetroot, cucumber and pumpkin – soak them in water for at least 12 hours. Then you will not have to wait so long for the seedlings to come up.

An easy way to plant small seeds

If you want to plant small seeds in a straight row, dip a piece of wet string (or natural fibre) into a packet of seeds. The seeds will cling to the string. Pull the string gently in a straight line and plant both string and seeds together. Give it a try next time you plant carrots or lettuce seed.

Thinning out your seedlings

If all the seeds you plant come up, you may need to thin them out. Plants need enough space in which to grow. If they are too close together, they compete with each other for food, water and light and they become weak and unhealthy.

After about four weeks, thin out the crowded seedlings so that you have the correct spacing (check the planting guide on pages 174–6 or use your hand measures) between those that are left. The thinnings can either be eaten in soups, stews or salads, or given to a friend or neighbour. You can also sell them, wrapped in wet newspaper to keep them fresh, or transplant them into another bed.

Thin out your seedlings twice to make up for any losses that you may have as the little plants grow.

First thinning

Do this when the seedlings have their first pair of true leaves (about 5 cm in height). This makes enough space for the remaining plants to grow.

Second thinning

This is when the plants are 10–12 cm high and have at least two pairs of true leaves, in addition to the seed leaves. Thin out to the correct spacing distance for the adult plant.

Transplanting – a few tips

When the young seedlings have grown too close together in the seed bed, or in the nursery, you will need to separate them and move them to the spot where they will grow to maturity. The little plants may experience this move as traumatically as when you've had major surgery and need to convalesce. It must be done very carefully in order not to set the seedlings' growth back.

- Seedlings are ready to transplant when they are about 10 cm high (roughly the length from the tip of your index finger to the knuckle) and have two or more pairs of true leaves in addition to the first pair of seed leaves.
- Do it in the late afternoon, on a rainy or cloudy day, never in the mornings or in the midday heat.
- Use the dibber to prepare your planting holes.
- Put some compost or vermi-compost into the holes.
- Wet the soil thoroughly in the seedling bed.
- Loosen the small plants with a small fork, taking care not to damage the roots. Keep as much soil as possible around the roots.
- Do not pick up the seedlings by the roots or stems. Handle them by their leaves.
- Plant the seedlings deeper than they were – right up to the first pair of leaves. This will help them to stand up and will encourage the formation of extra roots.
- Firm the soil around the plant with your fingers, and water gently.
- Protect the plant with a bit of mulch drawn up to it, but not touching the plant.
- Put a deep layer of mulch between the plants, but do not cover them.
- In summer, make a shade hat for the plant out of an old milk carton. Leave the hat on for two to three days, until the plant has recovered.
- If you want to protect your seedlings from the winter cold, make a mini-hothouse from a clear plastic bottle cut in half.
- If you have transplanted many seedlings into one bed, it is a better idea to make a shade net out of cloth or vegetable bags sewn together to cover the whole bed.

Not all seedlings can be transplanted. These include peas, beans, pumpkins, the melon and squash family, mealies, sweet-corn, potatoes and carrots. In fact, you will get the best results if you soak the bigger seeds overnight and plant them in the exact place where they are meant to mature.

Crop rotation

Plants from the same vegetable group do not grow in exactly the same place season after season. Except for tomatoes (which seem to do best when you let them grow in the same place year after year), you will get better results from your garden if you rotate your crops. This helps to keep the soil healthy and to prevent disease.

A good rotation cycle is to follow heavy feeders by light feeders by soil builders.

Garden records become essential because as soon as you have harvested your first planting, you must replant immediately, following the crop rotation guide.

Succession planting

If you plant your crops gradually, over a number of months, you will have a supply of fresh produce throughout the year. If you plant everything all at once, you will have too many vegetables and then nothing at all.

If you have enough space, prepare four beds or more.

Wait for three to four weeks after planting the first bed, then plant the second bed. Wait another three to four weeks after that, and so on.

Companion planting

Certain plants are very happy growing close to one another because they improve each other's health and well-being and protect each other from pest attack. Tomatoes, for example, secrete an alkaloid which repels certain cabbage pests, and marigold roots give off a powerful substance that repels nematodes (eelworms, which cause root knots and death). Also, because some plants are heavy feeders and some are light feeders, and some even give food to the soil, they thrive when growing together.

Companion planting is the best way of using a small space for maximum production, improving the soil, reducing pests and disease and growing healthy, happy plants. A diversity of plants provides the most effective pest repellent and fertiliser. Companion planting also helps to get the most out of your garden by planting different vegetables together so that they can make the best use of available sun, nutrients and space.

Plant lots of herbs in your garden

Use them to flavour your food so that you can cut down on salt in your diet. This may help you to control high blood pressure.

So, either plant fast-growing plants in between slow-growing ones or take a look at the shape of the plants. Large, bushy plants such as tomatoes can provide protection from scorching sun for low-growing, shade-loving plants like lettuce and spinach. It also means that you use all the space in the beds to maximum advantage.

Some examples for you to follow …

Good companions

- Lettuce and spinach are natural companions for tall plants like beans and tomatoes, because they grow well in the shade that is cast by their neighbours.
- Lettuce also grows well together with carrots and onions, as they have different growth habits.
- Onions and tomatoes may be planted close together, because onions have a shallow root and tomatoes are deep rooting.
- Shallow-rooting leeks are happy side-by-side with deep-rooting carrots.
- Short, compact cabbage and tall tomato are fine together.
- Plant alternating rows of beans and potatoes.
- Sprinkle radish seed among the lettuce. Radishes mature so quickly that you can pull them out before the lettuce grows too big.

- Turnips and peas are good for one another.
- Herbs such as oregano, marjoram and lemon balm have a beneficial effect on surrounding plants and their strong scent confuses insect pests.
- Plant marigolds near beans, celery, egg-plant, lettuce, peppers, squash and tomatoes as these are very susceptible to nematode injury.

Bad companions

Some plants have a harmful effect on one another and should not be grown together.

- Don't plant tomatoes near mealies, beans, peas, potatoes or radishes; nor should these plants be rotated as they attract the same pests.
- Climbing beans are not happy with members of the cabbage and onion family.
- Fennel is not good for beans and tomatoes. Most plants dislike growing with fennel.
- Celery and carrots should not grow together or follow one another – they attract the same pests.
- Onions interfere with the growth of beans and peas.
- Plants which sprawl all over the place, such as pumpkin, squash and nasturtiums, should have a place to themselves and not be planted together with others.

Before setting up your planting plan, consult the table on the pages 88 and 89.

Plastic cooldrink bottles and yoghurt containers make good plant labels

- Cut up the plastic containers with sharp scissors or a knife.
- Make a sharp point at one end so the label can be easily stuck in the ground.
- Alternatively, make them rectangular, poke holes through the middle top and middle bottom, and then thread a stick through. Or make a hole at one end and thread some string through it. Tie the label onto a stick.
- Use a permanent marker to write on the labels.
- And remember, they can be re-used when you replant after you have harvested.

Some more tips for successful gardening

- Start your crops off in seed trays or beds and transplant them into the garden when they are about 10 cm high. This means that the plants spend less time in the ground and you do not have to wait for one harvest before you sow the next. Therefore, you can grow more crops each season. It also means that frost-sensitive crops can be started off in a protected spot long before conditions are right for them outside; it gives them a head start.

- Plant cut-'n-come-again crops like spinach, bush and climbing beans, non-heading lettuces, Chou Mellier kale, parsley, rocket and baby marrows. One sowing may give you a year or more of harvesting, with no gluts or shortages. The more you pick, the more the plants produce.

- Pick the food from your garden when it is young and tender. Not only is it healthier for you, but it will increase the productivity of your plants. Whenever possible, eat it raw (cooked only by the sun; this will save on your electricity bills).

Start your crops off in seed trays

"Style [in your garden] has nothing to do with money. Anybody can do it with money. The true art is to do it on a shoestring."
TOM HOGAN

Know your plants' likes and dislikes: a few tips for companion planting

Vegetables	Likes	Dislikes
Asparagus	Tomatoes, basil	
Bush beans	Most vegetables, especially beetroot, carrots, celery, egg-plant, mealies, leeks, potatoes, strawberries, radish, cauliflower, cucumber, lettuce, marigolds, petunias, summer savory	Onions, garlic, chives, fennel
Climbing beans	Mealies, carrots	Sunflower, onions and the cabbage family
Beetroot	Bush beans, onions, kohlrabi, lettuce, crucifers, chives	Climbing beans
Cabbage family (including broccoli, Brussels sprouts, cauliflower, kale, kohlrabi)	Beetroot, celery, lettuce, onions, potatoes, tomatoes, bush beans, chamomile, dill, thyme, sage, oregano, marigolds, rosemary	Climbing beans, strawberries, garlic, rue
Carrots	Bush beans, lettuce, leeks, onions, peas, radish, tomatoes, climbing beans, parsley, dill, sage	
Celery	Bush beans, cabbage family (especially cauliflower), leeks, tomatoes	
Cucumber	Bush beans, cabbage family, celery, mealies, lettuce, radishes, sunflower, nasturtiums	Potatoes
Egg-plant (brinjal or aubergine)	Bush beans, pea, potatoes, nasturtiums	
Leeks	Beetroot, bush beans, carrots, celery, onions	
Lettuce	Carrots, radishes and lettuce are a very good combination; also onions, spinach, strawberries, chervil	
Mealies	All varieties of bean, beetroot, cucurbits (cucumber and squash family), potatoes	
Onions	Beetroot, cabbage family, carrots, lettuce, leeks	Peas, beans

Vegetables	Likes	Dislikes
Parsley	Basil, chives, asparagus, excels in the shade of tomatoes	
Peas	Carrots, radish, spinach, turnips	Potatoes, onions
Potatoes	Bush beans, cabbage family, mealies, peas, marigolds	Sunflowers, tomatoes, rosemary, cucumber, pumpkin, squash
Radish	Quick growing so interplant with most vegetables, beans	
Soya beans	Most vegetables, interplant with mealies	
Squashes and pumpkin family	Mealies and radish	Potatoes
Strawberries	Bush beans, onions, peas, spinach, lettuce, marigolds, borage	Cabbage family (Brassicas)
Sunflowers	Cucurbits, sweet-corn	Climbing beans, potatoes
Tomatoes	Asparagus, basil, celery, onions, cabbage family	Apricot trees, potatoes, fennel, strawberries
Turnips	Peas	
Zucchini (baby marrow)	Nasturtiums	

CHAPTER EIGHT

Fertilising the natural way

To make sure that your plants grow quickly and that they are healthy and succulent to eat, you need to feed them in three ways:

1 Give them a regular treatment with compost.

2 Add plenty of mulch continually to the surface of the beds (and a variety of different mulches at that).

3 Give your plants a dose of one or more of the following liquid fertilisers that you can make cheaply and easily in your backyard. Water the roots and the leaves with these "teas" once a week.

Start by recycling your home and garden waste through a compost heap.

Compost, or "black gold", is expensive to buy, but you can make it very easily in your garden, as long as you have enough space. You also have to make it correctly so that it doesn't attract rats and mice.

In the soft, warm bosom of a decaying compost heap, a transformation from life to death and back again to life is taking place ….

Did you know that only two out of every one hundred drops of water actually reach the roots of a plant? Yes, 98% is wasted through run-off and evaporation by the sun and wind.

What is compost?

In nature, decaying plants and animal remains are slowly changed into humus by millions of microbes in the soil. The process of composting in your backyard mimics nature. All the materials that you pile into a heap are converted rather more speedily into the sort of material you find on a forest floor: rich, dark, sweet-smelling and very fertile.

Compost is a dark, rich soil-building ingredient that is rich in humus. It contains millions of micro-organisms that convert dead organic matter into humic acid, locking up the nutrients in very large molecules that are not readily water-soluble. This means that they do not get leached out of your soil as soluble fertilisers do and the nutrients are not "force-fed" to plants as they take in water. Plants can absorb and digest these nutrients with their feeder roots, taking in just what they need for healthy growth.

Compost is not just a natural fertiliser containing a "balanced meal" of minerals. It has been described as "a healing agent for the soil's wounds" by Wendy Johnson. You only have to fork it in to tired, depleted soil or spread it over bare patches in your lawn, to see the miraculous effect it has on plant growth. It adds essential nutrients and replaces the soil destroyed by years of abuse by thoughtless gardeners and farmers.

What else can compost do for you?

- It increases the soil's ability to hold water and therefore prevents the leaching of nutrients to the deeper soil layers.
- It improves drainage in heavy, clay soils.
- It increases biological activity in the soil. Microbes in compost increase the plants' immunity to diseases (compost "tea" suppresses fungal diseases) and controls disease organisms in the soil.
- Because compost improves the soil structure, it reduces erosion (soil loss) by wind, rain and run-off.
- It costs far less than commercial fertilisers and releases its nutrients as, and when, the plant needs them.
- Making compost contributes towards reducing your impact on the waste stream by recycling biodegradable waste.

Compost heaps are simply piles of plant and animal materials. If you keep the pile damp, the materials will decompose through a natural heating process and the work of soil micro-organisms. Making compost is a process of cultivating these particular micro-organisms. They need water, air, lots of carbon-rich food, not too much nitrogen food, micro-nutrients, an acid environment, and heat.

Things to consider when choosing a site for a compost heap ...

- The site must be sheltered from the wind and direct sunlight.
- Avoid trees with hungry roots, such as pines, acacias, gums, willows and poplars.
- A permanent site will encourage the build-up of desirable organisms in the soil beneath. They can then move quickly into new heaps and get on with their work of decomposition.

Materials to compost

Organic matter
Outdoor or garden refuse
Straw, untreated sawdust, hay, corn cobs, leaves, dried grass clippings, shredded twigs, shredded bark, pine needles, hedge trimmings, weeds, untreated wood shavings, seaweed, water weeds.

Indoor waste
Coffee grounds, tea bags and tea leaves, reject or spoiled garden produce, vegetable and fruit peels, egg shells, egg boxes, cardboard, paper, cotton wool, cotton and wool rags, scraps of leather, old leather shoes, dead flowers.

Nutrients
Stable, kraal or poultry manure, blood meal, bone meal, wood ash (not coal ash), plants with deep rooting systems (such as comfrey, lucerne, dandelion, yarrow), weeds (such as nettle, chickweed, and so on).

All of these materials are either:
Nitrogenous (with a high nitrogen content)

When on their own and not mixed with carbonaceous materials, they tend to putrefy and create bad smells. They include fresh animal manures, fish wastes, green plant materials, wet kitchen wastes, blood and bone meal. We generally describe them as being "green, wets".

or

Carbonaceous (with a higher carbon content)

Because they are more stable, they do not decompose as easily. They include all the brown, dry materials, such as straw, shredded prunings, sawdust and other wood waste, dried maize stalks, dead leaves, newspaper and cardboard.

In order to make compost successfully, you need a 50:50 mix of the two types.

Compost in the making

There are some materials that you need to avoid adding to your compost heap:

- Material thicker than 1 cm (you should shred or chop to speed up decomposition).

- Diseased or pest-laden materials, such as those with scale insects or fungal diseases.

- Pernicious weeds like nut grass (*uintjies*) and kikuyu grass roots. Live grass roots must be thoroughly dried in the sun first.

- Meat, bones, fish, grease and oil, eggs, cheese and other dairy products (these slow down decomposition and attract rats).

- Cooked kitchen scraps. These may putrefy and attract rats. Rather feed them to the birds, chickens or your dogs.

- Weed seeds.

- Seed and fruit pips (attractive to rodents).

- Bluegum leaves and shreddings are not attractive to micro-organisms.

- Sawdust from treated wood.

- The top growth of main crop potatoes. This should be burned after lifting the potatoes because it may infect the heap with potato blight spores.

- Cat, dog or human manure – it will most likely contain parasites and their eggs.

- Plastic, glass, polystyrene, foil, synthetic materials, coal ash, glossy and highly coloured paper and cardboard.

So where do you find enough organic waste for compost making?

- Keep a bucket in your kitchen or outside your back door for all your biodegradable household waste.

- Save all your garden refuse and arrange with your neighbours to collect theirs.

- Ask your neighbours, family members and friends to do the same for you. Encourage your community to recycle their waste in this way. Be a pioneer!

- Organise with garden services in your area to drop off their day's collection at your gate. Let them know exactly what you're looking for.

- Visit the local hotels, supermarkets, markets, cafés, fruit and vegetable shops. It's a good way to get to know people and to raise awareness of an alternative way of doing things.

- Collect leaves from streets and local wooded areas or your friends' gardens.

- If all else fails and you have a spare, unused corner in your garden, let the weeds grow and use them to add to the compost heap. Alternatively, grow your own comfrey, lucerne, yarrow and clover.

Building your compost heap

There are a number of ways of building a heap, but basically all fall into one of two methods:

Cool composting

This is where you continuously add biodegradable materials as and when you have them. The pile is not turned, which reduces the amount of work you have to do and the heap does not have to be built all in one go.

However, it takes longer for materials to decompose, problem animals may seek it out and, because no heat is generated in the process, weed seeds and pathogens are not destroyed.

Hot composting

This is a better process and produces a higher-quality end-product because weed seeds and pathogens are all killed off. The materials are placed in carefully constructed layers with a balance of carbon- and nitrogen-rich inputs. It takes roughly three months (sometimes less) to produce dark, rich compost.

However, it is far more labour-intensive and requires careful management to ensure correct moisture and temperature levels.

This is how you go about it:

1 Mark the spot where you want your compost heap – not smaller then one square metre (1 m x 1 m), not wider than 2 metres, and as long as you like. Make sure that the site is well drained. Water-logging in the rainy season means that air is excluded from the heap, leading to anaerobic conditions, bad smells and a poor end-product.

2 Loosen the soil to a depth of one or two spades. This will make it easier for earthworms and micro-organisms to enter your heap and will improve drainage and aeration.

3 Build a layer of about 20 cm of small branches, twigs, cabbage stalks and mealie cobs (all coarse materials that take a long time to break down). This will allow air to enter and circulate within the heap.

4 Place one or more poles in the middle so that they stand upright or place them horizontally. They may be removed once you have finished building the heap. This allows air in and out of the heap.

5 Make a layer (about 10 cm deep) of plant or kitchen waste on top of the twigs and small sticks.

6   Make the next layer of dry grass and broken-up crop wastes. Water this dry material before it is added to the heap. This layer should also be about 10 cm deep.

7   Make the next layer of soil about 25 mm deep. Add manure if you have any. If you do not have a lot of manure, it is a good idea to make a slurry of manure and water in a bucket and pour it over this layer.

8   Repeat steps 5, 6 and 7 five times or until your heap is at least 1,5 metres in height.

9   Sprinkle each section with water. Just dampen the heap – try not to soak it. It is important that you water as you go, and not afterwards, and test that the material is sufficiently damp by squeezing a handful. It should be like a moist sponge, whose water can just be squeezed out.

10 Cover the entire heap with about 5 cm of soil, or dry straw, or old carpet under-felt – basically anything that will allow the heap to breathe. Some people even use plastic to retain moisture and keep the temperature constant. This is a very useful thing to do in hot, dry areas, or where there is heavy rainfall. However, make sure that there is a space between the plastic and the heap for air circulation. This is very important.

11 A well-made heap will heat up and steam within 2–3 days and then gradually cool over some weeks. Insert a metal stake (a crude thermometer) to test for heat and moisture. The pile must be kept moist.

12 After about six weeks, the heap must be turned to re-stimulate the heating process. The temperature in the heap should reach 60–70°C. In autumn and spring, when biological activity is at its highest, the process will be speeded up and no turning will be necessary. The bigger the heap, the more frequently it needs to be turned.

The compost should be ready for use in about 8–12 weeks and may even take up to six months, depending on the season. It should have a sweet smell and be rich and dark-looking, with a certain sticky (or **colloidal**) quality. That is, if you squeeze it in the palm of your hand, it forms a spongy ball.

How to speed up the composting process

• Chop up the material with a spade before putting them into the heat. The smaller the pieces, the faster they will decompose.

• Add manure or urine to activate the composting process. A good idea in making any heap is to aim at 25% animal manure content. If you can't find enough manure, make what you have into a slurry and water each layer with it. Otherwise, urine is high in nitrogen, is easily collected and works just as well. Other materials which are suitable as compost activators are comfrey and yarrow.

• Add more green material than brown but don't overdo it.

• Keep the moisture content just right, like a damp sponge. If the heap is too wet, too dry or "dead" (non-active), it will not mature.

• Turn it over with a fork once the temperature has dropped – roughly every two to three weeks. The more you turn the heap, the faster it will decompose. Each time you turn it, the temperature will rise, and once the heat-loving microbes have completed their work, the temperature drops again.

• The heap must be well aerated so that oxygen is available to the organisms in the heap.

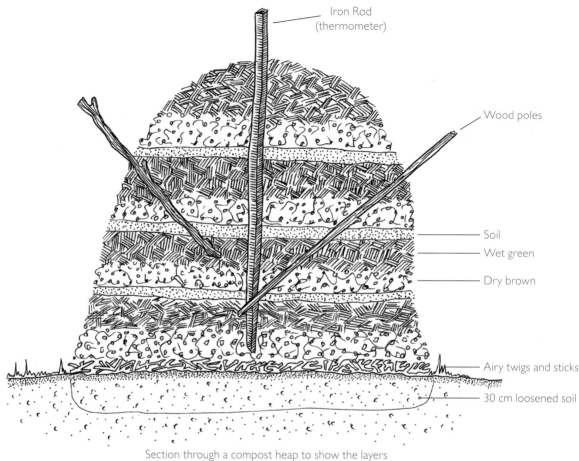

Iron Rod
(thermometer)

Wood poles

Soil

Wet green

Dry brown

Airy twigs and sticks

30 cm loosened soil

Section through a compost heap to show the layers

A couple of points to bear in mind …

A heap which is two metres long, one-and-a-half metres
high and one metre long will produce one cubic metre of
compost.

Use the compost as it becomes ready, or it will slowly
lose its nutrients. They can break down, dissipate into
the air or are leached out by rain. It may be dug in, or
used as a mulch or top dressing; it may also be sieved and
used as a medium for seed sowing. Any residue from the
old heap can form the base for the next heap. Remember:
it will be teeming with micro-organisms that are just
"rarin' to go"!

Some people add agricultural lime to their compost
heaps. If you use egg shells, bones, hoof and horn meal
or bone meal, it should not be necessary. Lime can be
a mixed blessing. It decomposes organic material very
quickly and can also "lock up" some of the plant nutrients
and cause imbalances. Also, many plants prefer a slightly
acid soil and therefore cannot tolerate the addition of
lime.

Making a fertiliser tea

Making a fertiliser tea

How much to use

- In your home vegetable garden, use one ten-litre bucket for every one square metre of bed.
- In a larger garden, use two cubic metres per 600 square metres.
- In a market garden, use 20 cubic metres per half a hectare.
- In vineyards and orchards, use 10 cubic metres per half a hectare per year.

Don't despair if you are unable to produce your own …

Firstly, if you have an established garden and not enough space for a compost heap, then keep a small hole open in your garden (half a metre square and half a metre deep).

- Heap the soil that you remove next to it.
- Start at one end of your garden and fill the hole with all your household biodegradable waste – just like the trench filling described earlier.
- Keep a small bucket in your kitchen and add all your vegetable waste, pot scrapings, rinse water from washing fruit and veggies, and so on.
- Once full, deposit in the hole and cover with soil to prevent flies getting at it.
- Continue doing this until the hole is full of organic waste and soil.
- Dig the next hole next to it, and so the story goes. This is an excellent way to increase the organic matter in your soil, with the minimum of effort.

Secondly, keep a few chickens, rabbits or ducks to eat your household waste. Their nutrient-rich manure will give your garden an instant boost and the chickens and ducks will also tackle any pest problems you may have.

Lawn clippings, leaves and small prunings make a very effective mulch. Make sure, though, that fresh green materials do not come in direct contact with the soil because they rob it of nitrogen as they start to decompose. Your plants will feel the pinch and start looking a yellow shade of green.

Start working with earthworms. These amazing creatures will gobble up your waste, turning it into the most valuable black, humus-rich substance that is full of nutrients – even more so than ordinary compost. Read Chapter 6 on earthworm farming and set one up outside your back door immediately. It's the answer to so many of the challenges we face today.

*Regular applications of compost or
well-rotted manure to the garden beds
boost the fertility of the soil by increasing
humus and nutrient levels.*

Liquid manures: a quick fix for sickly plants

Liquid manures (teas) are easy to prepare and can be used either to give a boost to plants that are not thriving, or to give young plants a boost during the first four to six weeks of growth.

Apply to the roots and to the leaves (as a foliar feed) once a week early in the morning before the sun heats up. They work quickly and give the plants a big boost. They can also be used for feeding perennials, shrubs, fruit trees and trees in a slightly higher concentration.

Manure tea
(contains a lot of nitrogen)
Fill a small hessian sack or an old plastic-mesh vegetable bag with manure and hang it in a bucket or a drum of water for about two weeks.

Quarter-fill a bucket or watering can with the liquid manure and add water to the top. The diluted mixture should be the colour of weak tea.

One ten-litre bucket of this manure "tea" is enough for one square metre of garden. Water the roots and the leaves of the plants.

Compost tea
(contains many different nutrients and is very good for seedlings and for helping your plants to fight disease)
Make this in the same way as for manure tea but soak for one night only. Mix half a bucket of tea with half a bucket of water.

Seaweed tea
(contains large amounts of all minerals plus other substances which stimulate root growth in plants – strong root systems are essential for healthy plants)
Collect, rinse and chop up some seaweed. Soak one bag of seaweed in a drum of water for one to two weeks.

Mix half a bucket of tea and half a bucket of water.

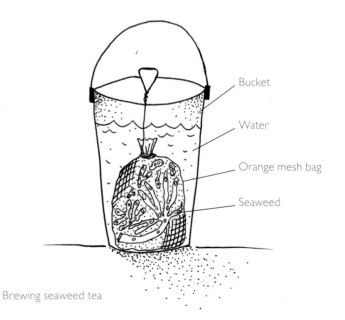

Bucket

Water

Orange mesh bag

Seaweed

Brewing seaweed tea

Comfrey tea

(mixed nutrients, and the best source of organic potassium)

There are a number of different methods for producing comfrey tea.

Place about half a kilogram of comfrey leaves in a ten-litre container and fill it up with water. Cover tightly. The comfrey goes black and ferments rapidly.

In about four weeks a clear liquid can be drained off.

Mix one part of the tea with one part of water. This is very good for tomatoes that are just beginning to fruit. Put the residue onto the compost heap.

Word of warning:
The smell of this brew is overpowering.
Arm yourself with a clothes-peg.

Use a 25-litre bucket with a tap, or a hole, at the bottom.

Pack the leaves into the bucket until it is crammed full and put a weight on top of them.

Put a lid on the bucket and a can underneath the tap or hole.

After about two weeks you will be able to collect a concentrated liquid, which should be diluted in the ratio of 25 ml of liquid to one litre of water. The concentrate stores well in a sealed bottle for later use.

This method is less smelly:

Mix half a kilogram of chopped comfrey leaves into ten litres of water and two litres of urine.

- Allow this mixture to ferment for two weeks.
- Strain the liquid off and dilute with water in the ratio of one part comfrey tea to ten parts water.

Nettles - your garden's miracle worker. Don't waste them.

They grow best in cool, shady places. Harvest the whole plant and use them to control pests, and feed your soil and your family. Stinging nettles *(brandnetel)* are delicious to eat and are rich in vitamins A and C. They contain protein, phosphorus, sulphur and traces of iron. They are used as fodder for livestock and a source of fibre for making cloth, rope and paper, for preparing green and yellow dyes for paper, for the preparation of homoeopathic remedies and as a hair tonic. The juice from nettles can be used in cheese-making as a substitute for animal rennet. In the garden, sprays made from nettle not only give plants some of the nutrients they need but also help to control pests and diseases. So save seeds from the nettles you find! Nettles grow best in cool, shady places. Once they have set seed, they start to look straggly. Cut back the plants and lay them on newspaper in a warm place. Once they are dry, shake them over the paper to release the seeds and store them in an airtight container ready for sowing in autumn.

Nettle pest-control spray is good for controlling snails and slugs as well as black spot and other fungal and viral diseases.

To make this spray, pack the nettles loosely into a large bucket. Cover with water and a lid (it gets a bit smelly) and let it stand for two weeks. Dilute one part of the resulting concoction with four parts of water; strain through a piece of old pantyhose or a sock and use as a general spray.

Nettle flowers

Stinging nettle tea

(phosphorus, sulphur and trace elements)

- Pack whole nettle plants (stems, roots, leaves and flowers) loosely into a large bucket.

- Soak up to 24 hours, no longer.

- Mix one part of the tea to one part water.

(Note the difference between this and the nettle spray for pest control – see page 111.)

Weed tea

(mixed nutrients)

Many weeds, such as dandelion and chickweed, have deep roots which take up valuable minerals from the subsoil and make them available for plant use. When these weeds are used as a mulch, dug into the ground, or added to the compost, they enrich the soil with these minerals and provide food for the vegetables that are growing.

Comfrey

Lucerne: a high-protein vegetable and a good crop for a quick winter and early summer harvest …

Most people think that lucerne is only for cows! But it is actually an important source of food for humans as well; rich in protein, vitamins and minerals. Cook it with spinach or beetroot leaves, or cabbage or turnip leaves. It is delicious and nutritious. Autumn and winter are the times to plant lucerne (the seed remains viable for up to five years) so that by the end of July you will be able to start harvesting the young tips. Add them to soups and stews or chop them into salads. You can also tie the tips into small bunches and hang them in a cool airy place to dry out. Crush the dried material into a glass jar, seal and keep as a sprinkle for your food. After harvesting continually for three months, cut the plants down to the ground in October, chop them into small pieces with a spade and dig them into the soil. Lucerne is a leguminous plant and this process of digging the plant remains into the ground is called green manuring. It makes the soil nitrogen-rich for the growing of the next crop of leafy vegetables such as spinach, cabbage and lettuce. No fertilisers necessary – nature does it for you.

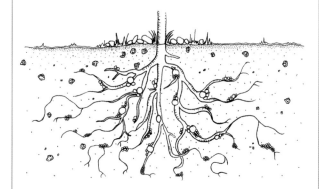

Nitrogen-fixing legumes should have nodules scattered throughout the root system. The more nodules the better. These are little fertiliser factories that fix nitrogen from the atmosphere into a soluble form that can be taken up by plant roots.

Make a weed tea by soaking the weeds that you pull up in a bucket of water, leaving them for a few weeks, straining the mixture through an old stocking and then watering your plants with the diluted tea.

Some useful weeds

There is a group of plants called **"dynamic accumulators"**. These are plants that generally have deep root systems and that actually search for nutrients lacking in soils, making them available for plant use. They are essentially the "miners" of the plant world. Not only are they useful additions to your garden and your compost heap, but many are an excellent supplement to your diet.

When is a plant a weed?
According to Edwin Rollin Spencer,
a weed is 'any plant that insists on growing
where the [gardener] wants another plant to grow.
It is a plant out of place in the eye of man;
in the eye of nature it is very much in place.'

Dandelion *(Taraxacum officinale)*
- Rich in minerals, particularly calcium and iron.
- The young leaves make an excellent addition to salads. They are high in vitamins A, B complex, C and E and the iron they contain is easily utilised by your body. Dandelion tea has a diuretic effect.
- Dried, roasted roots are ground into a caffeine-free coffee substitute.
- The flowers attract butterflies and birds and can be used to make jam.

Fat hen *(Chenopodium album)*
- Rich in calcium and iron.
- A good source of protein and vitamin B.

- Makes an excellent substitute for spinach in a variety of dishes.
- It attracts bees for pollination and hover flies which eat aphids.

Chickweed *(Stellaria media)*
- A good source of boron, which is essential for the transporting of sugar around the plant, for pollen formation (and, therefore, the fertility of the plant), and for maintaining the structure of the cell walls for healthy growth and development.
- It grows very rapidly and, because of its delicate stems and small leaves, will decompose very quickly. This makes it an excellent green manure crop.
- The seeds are much sought after by birds.

Black jack *(Bidens pilosa)*

> ## Black jack spray
>
> Cover a cup of ripe seeds with water and boil for 10 minutes. Alternatively soak them for 24 hours. Add one litre of water and a teaspoon of grated green bar soap dissolved in water. Spray immediately.
>   This spray stops insects from feeding, can kill some of them and acts as a repellent.

- The leaves are a good source of protein, calcium and zinc, and are rich in iron. They also contain selenium, which reduces free radicals in your body.
- Contains vitamins B, C and E and particularly high amounts of vitamin A, an immune-system booster. Young black jack leaves make an excellent addition to soup and stew pots, or steamed along with your spinach and other greens.
- The seeds make an excellent anti-pest spray.

Other "weeds" that you should look at with new eyes include stinging nettles, plantains, milk thistle, wild mustard, gallant soldier, bracken, clover and red pigweed. Many of these are used to make relish which you can add to *pap*, mealie rice, potatoes or soups and stews.

As you start reading, discussing and observing, you will be able to add to this list and you will cease to complain about weeds again.

The magic of mulch again

Perhaps the single most important activity of any gardener is to mulch the soil. Mulching conserves water, builds soil and saves you an enormous amount of time and effort. Yet converts to this gardening practice are few and far between. Two simple illustrations of Mother Nature in action should suffice to convince you of its importance.

The first is one of the lowly "weed" (dare I call it that?) commonly found growing on soil that has been bared for one reason or another – usually an act of man and bulldozer. Commonly known as *duiweltjies* or *dubbeltjiedoring* (*Tribulus terrestris*), you have possibly seen it on roadsides and waste ground.

It is a small, prostrate annual plant, with a deep tap-root system from which the stems spread out. Its growth habit is such that the plant appears to be protecting the soil. The delicate leaves and flowers complete their earthly tasks very quickly. Having accumulated minerals and food reserves and produced seeds for future generations, they quickly die, dry out and are left on the soil surface to cover and protect it further, to provide organic matter for incorporation into the soil and also to create a little niche for the seed of some other plant to settle in and take root.

The roots of the *duiweltjies* seek out nutrients in the depths of the soil and bring them up to the surface, where they are deposited when the leaves die. These plants are pioneers in the true sense of the word. They prepare barren soil for a host of other plants that will surely follow once the "spadework" has been done. Plant pioneers protect it while they're alive and, in death, deposit a minuscule layer of mulch which will break down, releasing nutrients into the top soil layers.

Leaf mould: a valuable commodity in the garden

Autumn leaves are a real bonus to the home gardener. Rake them up and put them in heaps, preferably in a wire mesh enclosure, in a corner of your garden. Alternatively you can put them into black garbage bags, add a little water, seal them and forget about them for a year or so. The process can be speeded up by mixing the dry leaves with fresh lawn clippings or manure at a rate of one part of clippings or manure, to four parts of leaves.

Fungi decompose the leaves in a long, cool process that is quite different from composting and so it is a good idea to keep them separate from the compost heap. Leaves have very little nutrient value, but the resulting leaf mould is an incredible soil conditioner and a mulch. It is good for creating a fine tilth in seed beds and can act as a replacement for peat as an ingredient in seedling and potting mixes.

Secondly, with the onset of autumn, deciduous trees prepare for the winter by withdrawing food reserves from their leaves and slowly but surely depositing these carbonaceous accessories on the ground beneath them. Mother Nature, in all her wisdom, is preparing for temperature extremes. The thick leaf layer is multi-purpose:

- It protects the root system from excessive cold and heat.
- The leaf mould that forms beneath a tree improves the structure of the soil, keeping it loose, aerated and well-drained.

- The leaf litter is broken down – together with flowers and fruits, branches and cones – by hordes of plants, animals and microbes, and the trapped nutrients are released into the soil. All summer, the plant has been bringing up minerals from the bowels of the earth. What we call "autumn" and the North Americans call "fall" sees these nutrients left behind on the surface of the Earth, to be utilised by other plants.

Mulching also prevents soil compaction and the crusting of the soil surface by absorbing the impact of falling rain drops.

Under many trees, the fallen leaves suppress the germination of seeds and the subsequent growth of plants that would compete with them for water and nutrients. Many little creatures can be found in this layer of matter. It provides them with habitats or places to live.

In the context of your garden, a layer of brown, dry material covering your soil is called "mulch". It too has many functions, all of them vitally important. In addition to those mentioned above, its role in water conservation is important. Mulch significantly reduces the evaporation of water from the soil surface and also protects it from the drying effects of the sun and wind.

Stone mulching around fruit trees and perennial plants will prevent chickens and guinea fowl from scratching and disturbing the mounds or basins built around plants. First add a layer of dry grass clippings and then put the stones in place.

An added benefit of the stones is that the crevices between the stones provide a place for spiders, frogs and lizards which will control the pests on your plants.

Since one is also growing a garden for food, mulching also reduces the number of weeds that come up between your plants. Weeds compete with your plants for sunlight, water and nutrients and mean ongoing work. You could be enjoying other aspects of your gardening experience instead of pulling up weeds.

Not to be glossed over is the role that mulch plays in building soil fertility. In a well-mulched garden, the soil below the mulch will be dark, damp and rich, teeming with life, most of which is too small to be seen with the naked eye. However, you will be familiar with woodlice, earthworms, millipedes, spiders, lizards, frogs, small snakes and the white threads of Actinomycetes. These organisms are evidence of the miraculous recycling of nutrients and energy that is going on in this little piece of heaven. Mulching is one of the simplest ways to build soil. Make it a routine and you'll see a major change in your garden's health and well-being in a very short space of time. As the mulch is broken down, add more. Just keep at it – regularly and frequently.

Mulching materials

Dry grass clippings, pine needles, straw, mealie cobs, coffee grounds, newspaper, cardboard, dry leaves, partially decomposed compost, untreated wood shavings, wood chips, chipped bark, stones and pebbles, ground shells, poultry and stable litter, seaweed, nut shells.

Living mulches include your plants, especially the ones that have a spreading growth habit. New Zealand spinach is one of these, as are other ground cover plants. The dense mat it forms over the surface is the ultimate soil protector. And remember too that, with correct soil preparation, your plants will be growing close enough to be touching one another. The canopy that this creates is also a very effective "living mulch".

CHAPTER NINE

Controlling plant pests and diseases the natural way

If you've followed all the guidelines in this book for setting up a food garden, you're already on the road to harvesting your bounty: safe, fresh, delicious and nutritious. And plenty of it from a small patch of rich and healthy soil. You've already given yourself a new lease on life by experiencing the warmth of the sun on your skin, the wind in your hair and the pleasure of pure physical exhaustion followed by deep, relaxed sleep.

Unfortunately, your efforts will also have boosted the populations of butterflies, moths, snails and grasshoppers, and the invisible spores of the microbes that appear like magic for their share of the harvest. Curb the urge to rush to the nearest nursery for a bottle of "antidote". Remember the consequences of your actions and rather contemplate Mother Nature's apothecary.

When your plants look sick, or are damaged,
it is important to understand what caused
the problem, and to know how to deal with it
without resorting to poisons.

It all starts with the soil.

If you have healthy soil, you will grow healthy plants, and so pests and diseases are less likely to be a problem in your garden. Follow the *Golden Gardening Rules*, create a healthy environment, and remember that:

Prevention is better than cure …

The Golden Gardening Rules

1. **Build healthy soil**

   Soil that is rich in organic matter and full of living creatures will produce healthy plants which resist attack. To improve the soil, dig less, mulch more and use loads of compost.

2. **Plant in the right season**

   Consult a planting guide for your area. If you expose your plants to climatic conditions for which they are not suited, they will become stressed and therefore more prone to pests and disease.

3. **Don't overcrowd your plants**

   Sow thinly, then thin the seedlings out. Transplant the thinnings to other areas in your garden, or else add them to your salad or soup pot. Delicious and nutritious.

4. **Plant a big variety of plants in your garden**

   Most plants like to help each other, so get to know their likes and dislikes. This will encourage more animal life in your garden and create a good balance of pests and their predators. Remember that every strand in the web of life is important. There really are no "bad guys"; it just looks that way because your system is out of balance.

5 Rotate your crops

A (legumes and maize) → B (leaf and fruit crops) →
C (root crops) → A → B → C.

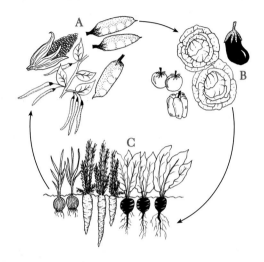

6 Never use poisonous sprays and artificial fertilisers in your garden

Rather encourage a well-balanced eco-system. Do not destroy all pests, even the "bad" ones. A balance is very important.

7 Provide a variety of habitats

This will encourage frogs and lizards, snakes and birds, spiders, praying mantids and chameleons (the predators) that eat the "bad guys".

Know what is causing the problem in your garden

It is not necessary to know the scientific name of every type of pest and disease which could occur in a garden. So many different types exist that this would be almost impossible. What is important, though, is to know:

• whether your plants have been attacked by a pest

• whether they have a disease

A paper wasp on her nest made of wood pulp and saliva. The young are fed on a diet of chewed-up caterpillars.

Daddy Long Legs spiders prey on ants and other garden pests. Encourage them to take up residence in your garden.

Honey bees are essential for pollination and thus for the production of seeds and fruits.

- are suffering from a nutrient deficiency
- or have simply been damaged by wind, hail and the likes.

How would you identify the root of your problem?

Pests include any animals that do damage to your garden: various bugs, caterpillars, insects and eelworms, birds, cats, dogs, livestock and even human beings. They can live on the bits of your plant, above and below the ground, and can be divided into groups, identified by the type of damage they do.

Insect pests, for example, either chew or bite, bore or suck juices from plants. Each different method can be identified by the damage that it does to the plant.

Nutrient deficiencies or starvation problems

As we saw on pages 44 and 45, plants require the major nutrients (nitrogen, phosphorus and potassium) in large amounts. They also need other nutrients and trace elements (like magnesium, manganese, iron, boron, molybdenum, copper and zinc) in much smaller amounts.

If these materials are not in the soil, plants show all sorts of signs. For example, if there is a shortage of nitrogen in the soil, plant growth is stunted and the leaves are pale green and small.

Nutrient deficiencies result in weak, sickly plants, which are more likely to be attacked by pests and diseases.

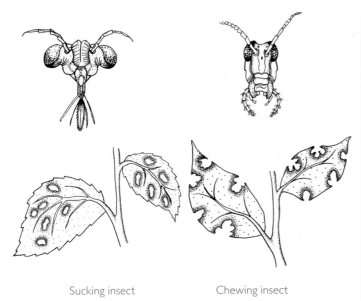

Sucking insect   Chewing insect

Shadecloth offcuts make good windbreaks

Diseases are more difficult to identify. Plants can suffer from fungal, viral or bacterial diseases, but you are more likely to come across fungal diseases, as these are the most common.

Something else to think about …
How many of your plant problems
are caused by …

- A lack of water or drought? This causes browning of the leaves, wilting and leaf fall.

- Over-watering? The main signs of this are yellowing and wilting of the leaves.

- Too much shade? Plants grow tall and spindly.

- Heavy rain and hailstorms that tear holes in the leaves and damage flowers and fruits?

- Frost, which freezes and burns leaves, flowers and fruits?

- Excessive wind? Shredded leaves and broken branches can be avoided by building or growing windbreaks around the garden.

Windbreaks not only deflect the wind, but also help to conserve water.

What do you do if the garden attack gets out of control?

If you've followed all the golden rules and some of your plants are still being attacked by pests and diseases, there are safe ways to protect them.

Go the natural route …
There are many different ways of tackling the problems
that beset you. Work them all together for best results. And
remember: if you take the organic route, you need to work at
it. Don't give up on day two!

Caterpillar of the common Painted Lady butterfly

Start the journey which will restore the balance and bring Nature into her full glory.

Take the journey step by step.

Step 1: Build the soil.

Step 2: Plant the largest possible variety of plants.

Step 3: Provide a variety of habitats in your garden.

Step 4: *Never* be tempted to use poisonous chemicals and artificial fertilisers in your garden.

Diatomite

Otherwise known as "diatomaceous earth", diatomite is a fine, grey powdery material made up of the 30 million-year-old shells of microscopic water plants.

The shells (exo-skeletons) of diatoms are made of silica, almost like little glass houses. When alive, they float in the top layers of water of oceans and lakes, playing an important part in food chains and webs. When they die, their bodies sink to the mud at the bottom where they decay, leaving behind the glassy shells which last forever.

The powder, when sprinkled on plants and soil, acts like a million tiny razor blades on soft-bodied pests such as the caterpillar of the cabbage white butterfly, scratching its body as it crawls over it. This results in the creature drying out and dying.

Some facts about diatomite:

- It does not kill instantly.
- It acts on most pests only when they are in their larval, maggot or grub stage, when their skins are soft. It does not harm earthworms.
- It doesn't work so well in wet weather, because the insects don't dry out.

How to use it

- Use an old talcum-powder bottle or make a dusting bottle from a plastic tub with a screw-on lid. Use a red-hot darning needle to burn lots of holes in the plastic lid.
- Dust the plants by shaking the bottle over the soil and plants.
- Dust around the base of the plant in the late afternoon/early evening.
- For best results, spray the plants first and then dust from the bottom up.
- Make sure that you dust the stem and both the top and under surfaces of the leaves.
- You will need to dust again after rain.

Warning: Be careful not to inhale the powder.

Diatomite can also be applied wet

- Add one tablespoon of grated kitchen soap to a litre of boiling water.
- Let it dissolve and then add this soapy solution to a bucket.
- Increase it to about 20 litres with cold water.
- Put about 200 g of diatomite into the bucket and mix well.
- Keep stirring the mixture as you spray.

Where to get it

First of all, never, ever use diatomite that is meant for swimming pool filters. Apparently, it is specially treated for this specific purpose and may be carcinogenic. Rather ask your local nurseryman to order some for you.

Controlling pests the natural way

Some general tips

- Use your eyes to spot the pests and your hands to remove them.
- Check your garden on a daily basis so that things don't get out of control.
- Invest in a magnifying glass and start spying on things. Once the sun sets and darkness descends on your garden, a whole new world comes alive. Get out there and start investigating those little critters. Night-time is feeding time and also a fascinating time to learn about the inhabitants of your space on the planet.
- Crushed eggshells around plants help to deter snails and slugs.
- You can also try the wonder compound, diatomite, which works like a charm on any soft-bodied insects.

The more you learn, the more you realise
how little you know ...

Garlic soap spray

- Crush 10 cloves of garlic with a quarter cup of grated kitchen soap and soak this in one litre of boiling water.
- Once it is cool, spray on the leaves of those plants which have insects on them.
- Repeat one week later.
- This spray is also good for controlling fungal infections.

Chilli spray

- Cut four chillies, one onion and two cloves of garlic into small pieces.
- Make a light lather using kitchen soap and mix with water.
- Cover the cut chillies, onion and garlic with a little of the soapy water.
- Let the mixture stand for 24 hours.
- Add one litre of water and mix well.
- Strain through an old stocking and seal in a bottle.
- Spray onto plants when necessary.

(There is a detailed discussion on chilli sprays in the box on page 112.)

More natural methods you can try

Onion spray is a fungicide, an insecticide and an insect repellent. Chop one medium-sized onion into small pieces (use the skin and green leaves as well, if you have them). Soak in one litre of water in a closed container for between four to seven days. Strain the mixture through an old stocking and spray onto the affected plants.

Make a tea with a few flower heads of **pyrethrum** (*Chrysanthemum coccineum)* or **feverfew** in one litre of water. Add a little soap. Use in the evenings to control aphids, caterpillars, leafhoppers, mites, thrips, mildew and scab. Pyrethrum is poisonous, and should only be used as a last resort.

Nettles make an excellent spray for snails and downy mildew. Pack whole nettle plants into a bucket. Cover with water and leave to stand for two weeks. Dilute one part of the liquid with four parts of water, and spray. This spray is made differently to the nettle fertiliser.

Black jacks are annual weeds with clusters of spiky black seeds that most of us have seen when they stick to our trouser legs. They make an excellent spray for pests – either by stopping the insects from eating, killing them or simply repelling them. The spray can be used against aphids, ants, beetles and caterpillars. To make a spray, all parts of the plant can be used, particularly the ripe seeds. Chop the plant parts and cover them and the seeds with water. Boil for ten minutes (or soak for 24 hours), allow to cool and add one litre of water and a teaspoon of soap. Shake well and spray immediately.

For **cabbage caterpillar dust**, mix two handfuls each of wood ashes and flour with half a cup of salt. Dust the plants to kill the caterpillars. Diatomite also works well.

Garlic, onion and chilli spray

Roughly chop a full hand of garlic and four onions, including skins.

Add a tablespoon of crushed, dried or fresh chilli or chilli seeds or one teaspoon of chilli powder.

Pour over 3 litres of boiling water, close the container and allow to stand for one day. Add 2 tablespoon of cooking oil and 2 tablespoons of liquid soap. Mix well.

- This spray is antibiotic, antiseptic and a broad spectrum fungicidal and insecticidal and will also kill beneficial insects. Therefore use it with great care, only spraying in the late afternoon/early evening.
- Do not spray too much as it can burn tender plants. Rather dilute if necessary.
- Spray at two or three day intervals.

Dilute one cup of this mixture with five cups of warm water and place in a spray canister. Before applying, check whether the spray is not too strong by spraying one or two leaves to see how they react. Wait for some hours. If necessary dilute further.

This spray is suitable for all plants that are being attacked by any of the following insects:

Aphids, cabbage butterfly, mites, scale, thrips, tomato flies, green fly, white fly, caterpillars, cutworms, red spider, all kind of beetles, all kind of moths, ants, termites, slugs and snails.

Do not use this spray on leguminous plants.

Because of the high sulphur content of the onions and the garlic it can also be applied to fungal, bacterial and blight attacks.

As this spray kills also beneficial insects, use only when absolutely necessary. And spray in the later afternoon/early evening to protect them.

Wormwood (*Artemesia absinthum)* **tea** repels aphids, flea beetles, flies, cabbage white butterflies and slugs, and can also be used as a bath to chase fleas from domestic pets. Make a tea by pouring one litre of boiling water over a handful of wormwood.

Collect the pests! Snails, beetles, caterpillars, whatever, and drop them into a tin of water to drown. Then pour hot water over them to make a strong "bug juice". Leave for five days. Strain off the liquid and use as a spray. No creature likes the smell of its own dead.

Try traps and scares before anything else. For example, tinfoil pie dishes and old CDs scare off birds.

Foil pie dishes make good bird scares.

An **Epsom-salts spray** helps plants with yellowing leaves after a viral attack, which is often brought on by sucking insects such as aphids. Such plants are deficient in magnesium. This may have been caused by the overuse of wood ashes, lime or phosphorus. Dissolve 50 g of Epsom salts in four litres of water and use as a foliar and root feed.

TIP: To make your sprays stick to plants:
Add a teaspoon of sugar or a little grated
kitchen soap to the spray.

P.S. Beer is bad for snails …

Did you know that beer is lethal for snails? Put a pot of beer in your garden to attract them. They'll climb in for the party but will never come out.

And just think about your early-morning cup of coffee. The lift-off feeling that it gives you is fatal to tiny insects. Make up a weak solution: try one teaspoon of coffee grounds per litre of hot water. Let it cool and zap them.

These are just a few ideas for tackling the problems caused by an imbalance in your garden system. Visit your local bookstore and start reading up on this fascinating topic.

Working with Mother Nature is exciting. She has more than a few tricks up her sleeve.

You need to keep on learning when you choose the natural route.

Controlling garden pests by using their natural enemies and diseases

*Garden pests and their natural enemies co-exist
in balanced populations in well-managed
organic gardens. All you have to do is sit back and
let them get on with life, and you won't have a problem with
losing your crops to the "bad guys".*

Nearly half of all the food produced in the world today is lost to insects, despite the dramatic increase in the use of pesticides. In 1945, when pesticide use was very low in the USA, maize-crop losses were around 3.5 percent. In the late 1990s, with one thousand times more pesticides being used, crop losses were estimated at 12.5 percent (Pimentel, 1995).

Little progress has been made in the war against insects because they are developing immunities to pesticides, and because the natural predators and parasites are being destroyed along with them. So, when you see some bugs in your veggie patch and you spray them with poison, it backfires on you. In a few days, or a few weeks, the same kind of bug is back again but, this time, there are more of them than before. Why does this happen?

You accidentally killed off the pest's natural enemies along with the pest. What's more, you cannot always kill off all the pests in your own garden and you cannot spray the neighbourhood gardens that may harbour them. So, without any natural predators or parasites to hold them in check, those pests that didn't die, or those that flew in from elsewhere, are able to multiply without restriction. Natural enemies do not usually reappear as quickly as the pest and some insecticides are more toxic to predators and parasites than to the pests.

At the same time, pests quickly develop resistance to the poison sprays. Individual insects have different levels of resistance to the sprays. Every time you spray an insect population, you change the balance between susceptible and resistant individuals. Obviously, the resistant individuals survive and reproduce while most of the susceptible ones die.

So it follows logically that the more pesticide you use to control the seeming problem, the faster you produce a population of resistant pests and the faster you lose your entire crop.

There is some good news though…

Convert your gardening methods to an organic approach and at least two-thirds of your pest problems will disappear. Don't be tempted to think "What can I use instead…?" or "What if …?" This is the wrong approach. Rather think along the lines of avoiding pest problems by managing your gardening correctly. This is about good gardening practices such as building healthy soil, planting mixed crops, following crop rotations and seasonal plantings, companion planting, using resistant varieties, creating physical barriers and/or traps, and creating habitats for frogs, lizards and birds.

Allow your garden to take control of itself and populations of natural enemies will re-establish themselves. Pest problems will become history.

What are the pests' natural enemies?

There are three types of natural enemies:

1 **Predators which eat insects**

Predators include spiders, wasps, praying mantids, lacewings, dragonflies and ladybirds (but watch out for the impostor ladybirds that have turned vegetarian and that attack potatoes, beetroot, spinach and members of the pumpkin family).

Each predator can eat hundreds, even thousands, of insects in a lifetime. Some, like spiders, have been shown by scientific analysis of their stomach contents to eat a wide variety of insects. For example, money spiders (*Lynyphiidae*) are prized by farmers in the United Kingdom because of their voracious appetite for aphids. But aphids have little nutritional value and spiders need to eat other insects to balance their diet. Predatory insects (and arachnids) do not damage crops.

2 **Parasites**

Most of these are insects that lay their eggs inside the body of a living insect, called a host. The parasite feeds on its host until it finally kills it. Then the adult parasite emerges from the dead host and searches for more insects to lay its eggs in. Using parasites is a slower way to kill pests but it is effective. There are many examples of insect parasites in your own (unsprayed) garden. Take the time to find some of them.

3 **Diseases carried by viruses and fungi that infect insects**

Diseases that directly affect the insect pests in your garden are carried by the insects themselves and can therefore wipe out whole populations very quickly. For example, when caterpillars are a problem you can use a Bt spray which contains *Bacillus thuringiensis*, a soil-borne bacterium harmless to human beings and animals. The Bt bacterium produces a toxin which, when ingested, causes the caterpillars to stop feeding, become ill, and die. It is lethal to a variety of insects, particularly the larval forms of moths and butterflies and is quoted as being about 90% effective.

The Cabbage White butterfly (*Pieris brassicae*) is a common sight in the vegetable garden and illustrates a number of examples of biological control in action. This species was accidentally introduced to the Western Cape from Europe (first sightings were reported in 1994) and it has since become a significant pest, particularly to small-scale farmers and home gardeners.

Its green, black and yellow larvae cause a lot of damage to the mustard family (*Cruciferae*), particularly cabbage, broccoli, cauliflower and rocket, and also to nasturtiums. Interestingly its preferred local food plants are also introduced species. The butterfly tolerates both hot and cold weather, seems unperturbed by the raging south-easters, and broods continually throughout the year, laying up to 125 eggs at a time. Populations surge in the cold months.

Mother Nature, having been left to her own devices, however, has deftly stepped in with a few

nifty solutions for its extermination, or at least to keep its population in check:

Argentine ants – aggressive aliens – have been observed to feed on, and carry away, the first instar (or newly hatched) larvae. One sure way to curb population growth.

Two species of **Tachinid fly larvae** have been recorded as parasitising the Cabbage White caterpillars. The adult looks like a small hairy housefly and survives on the nectar of flowers, but the larvae live as parasites on other insects. They do this in one of two ways:

Small, white, oval eggs are laid on the outside of a caterpillar of another species. The eggs hatch into tiny maggots, which bore into the living victims and devour them – first the body juices, then the fat, and finally the vital organs. The victim succumbs, and

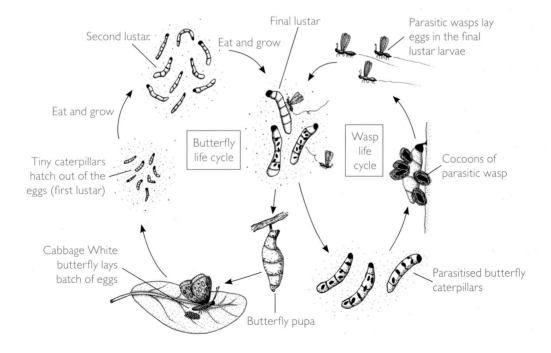

The Cabbage White butterfly population is controlled by a tiny parasitic wasp, *Pteromalus puparum*.

eventually only one brawny, hairy adult tachinid emerges. The other maggots were out-competed.

Other tachinids lay lots of tiny eggs on the surface of food plants and these are swallowed by grazing caterpillars. The emerging maggots bore through the gut wall and proceed to feed, leaving the poor victim's vitals to the end. In order to get the air they require, they pierce the body wall of the host and send their own breathing tubes to the surface or connect directly to the respiratory apparatus of the caterpillar.

If you have a vegetable patch you may have noticed butterfly pupae attached to the wall of your house. Periodically you'll have the joy of watching the crumpled adult emerge, blow up its wings and take off into the garden.

Often however, these cocoons remain intact; nothing ever comes out of them. That is a sign that Nature is at work or, should I say, that **wasps**, *"eco-warriors"* in the caterpillar war, are doing their job.

Cabbage White populations are checked by a tiny, indigenous, parasitic wasp, *Pteromalus puparum*. The female wasp lays her eggs in the body of the final larval stage of the caterpillars and her grubs feast on the tissues of the host. They follow the same pattern of consumption as the Tachinid maggots, attacking the nervous system last of all. It would be unwise to kill the host before the grubs are fully developed. The caterpillar remains alive and fresh, until just before the wasp grubs are ready to pupate and then they start nibbling at the brain. This brings about changes in the caterpillar's behaviour and it leaves the food plant and migrates up any vertical surface in the vicinity, in a premature attempt to pupate.

The wasp grubs finally kill the ailing caterpillar, and emerge to spin tiny cocoons covered in a golden net which will protect the pupating wasp larvae from attack by other parasites. Clusters of these cocoons can often be seen on vertical structures in and around your garden and home. You would have to be very observant to notice the little black wasps that emerge from them to continue their life cycle.

Unfortunately, as was mentioned earlier, populations of the Cabbage White butterfly increase quite dramatically in autumn and winter because the wasps do not tolerate the cold quite as well, and their activity levels are reduced. As the saying goes, "When the cats are away, the mice do play."

So successful are the techniques that some of these insect warriors are being shipped around the world. Overseas, you can buy them from mail-order catalogues and fly them into your own garden, orchard, small holding or farm: ladybirds, lacewings, wasps, praying-mantid egg cases – they're all in demand. A cup or two of ladybirds would be enough for the average garden and give them a balanced diet, too, because they feast on a huge variety of adult insects and larvae. Lacewing larvae have an insatiable appetite and can consume a few hundred aphids every two hours. Who needs poisons with allies like these?

Encourage the natural enemies to your garden by growing many different food crops and herbs and by keeping trees, shrubs and flowers growing around the boundaries. Apply organic fertilisers and loads of compost instead of nitrogen fertilisers. Experiment with different natural sprays and repellent crops. The important thing is that you try different techniques and find the best ones for your situation. In the end you will discover the best programme for managing any problems that arise in your garden.

Using natural methods to prevent outbreaks of disease

- **Use plants that are resistant** to the fungal diseases that are common in your area.
- Because fungal and bacterial spores germinate best in warm, wet conditions, try to reduce the times when plant leaves are wet. **Plant in sunny sites** with gentle wind.
- **Regular pruning** keeps the plants open, allowing air and sun to quickly dry branches and leaves after the rain or morning dew.
- **Crop rotation** helps to starve out the disease-causing organisms in the soil.

A low-cost, yet effective, spray bottle

- **Practise good garden hygiene**. Diseased plants should be burnt or put in the rubbish bin. Do not put them in the compost heap. Use the ashes as a fertiliser. Ash is high in potassium, which promotes good root growth and flower and fruit formation.

In the event of an outbreak, try one or more of the following remedies…

- **Onion spray** is a fungicide, an insecticide and an insect repellent. Chop one medium-sized onion into small pieces (use the skin and green leaves as well if you have them) and soak in one litre of water in a closed container for between four to seven days. Strain the mixture through an old stocking and spray onto the affected plants.
- **Garlic** has the same effect as onion. Crush one garlic bulb and add one litre of warm water. Shake well, strain, mix in a little liquid soap, and use immediately.
- Vigorously stir one heaped tablespoon of **wood ash** into one litre of water. Leave overnight, strain to remove solids and mix with one cup of sour milk and add three litres of water. Spray.
- Try adding one teaspoon of **bicarbonate of soda** and a teaspoon of liquid soap to a litre of water. This is a very good spray for fungal diseases.
- Another good option is to dilute one part of **milk** with nine parts of water and spray.

Important notes

- Use your eyes and hands first!
- Try traps and scares before anything else. For example, tinfoil pie dishes scare off birds.

A lethal flying machine: a dragonfly is a voracious predator

- Please remember that natural ways of controlling pests and diseases often require repeated use in the beginning. One-off sprayings will not work.

- When you go the organic route, there are two defences against pests and diseases: a healthy soil deals with 90% of the problems; the remaining 10% can be treated with a variety of practices.

- Diseases and pests are signs of imbalance within the whole garden system and are not an excuse to destroy a species and harm countless others with chemical poisons. Our approach therefore has to be to restore balance to the whole, while causing minimal damage to other parts of the web of life.

- Many of the control mechanisms are "invisible": crop rotation, companion planting and caring for the local ladybirds, praying mantids, lizards, frogs and birds. Other measures include changing sowing times, using resistant varieties, practising good garden hygiene, checking on pH levels in the soil and using organic sprays. These are non-synthetic sprays that rapidly break down in the biological cycles in the soil.

- Recognise that all creatures are actually your friends.

- Read, read and read. You have to keep on learning when you choose the organic route.

Whatever you do, don't use poisons in your garden: they kill the good guys, as well as the bad guys, have a lasting effect on the soil, and poison you as well.

Here are some common garden problems

Use these signs to tell you what has attacked your plants...

Numerous irregular holes in leaves are usually caused by caterpillars or adult and larval beetles. Examine both sides of the leaves and remove (or squash) the culprits. Very small beetles may chew only part of the way through the leaf and leave see-through windows. Sprinkle leaves lightly with wood ash.

Skeletonised leaves also result from insects eating between the veins. The usual culprits are beetles and their larvae.

Large irregular holes in leaves – snails and slugs are the most likely offenders. Check for their slimy trails as they feed at night. If there is no sign of these, look for grasshoppers.

Curled, very distorted leaves – aphids are the most common cause, especially on the young leaves at the ends of branches. Soap sprays help but very badly infested leaves should be removed and destroyed. Attract ladybirds to your garden by planting flowers and yarrow and leaving weeds like dandelion. Ladybirds eat aphids by the thousands. If the damage is mild, it may have been caused at bud stage and the pest may be gone.

Large areas eaten from leaves – grasshoppers and locusts are to blame. Plants may be completely stripped of leaves in severe cases. Birds, frogs and ground beetles usually control these predators.

Blotches or snaky patterns on leaves – leaf miners are small larvae that burrow between the top and bottom surfaces of a leaf, causing a blistering effect. Destroy badly affected leaves. To catch the adult before it lays eggs on the leaves, hang a strip of yellow plastic (or a piece of wood or cardboard painted bright yellow) above your plants. Smear it with Vaseline or something sticky. The flies will be attracted to the yellow colour and are trapped before they do the damage.

Mottled leaves – a sign of nutrient deficiencies often caused by sucking insects such as aphids. When aphids pierce plant tissue they often inject viruses which cause disease, apparent by the mottling of leaves.

Companion planting creates diversity in the garden

Use the aromatic properties of herbs to attract beneficial insects or to deter the harmful ones. This not only confuses pests, causing them to move away from your vulnerable crop, but also affects insects in such a way that they lay fewer eggs.

The following list gives you some information on which herbs will help you to control insect problems:

Problem	Herb
Ants	Pennyroyal, tansy, mint, garlic, lavender
Aphids	Basil, garlic, onions, chives, spearmint, lavender, nasturtium
Beetles	Rosemary, garlic chillies
Cabbage White butterfly	Dill, sage, oregano, tomatoes, mint, thyme
Eelworm	Marigold
House flies	Basil, rue, tansy
Fruit flies	Rue, tansy
Mice	Garlic
Mosquitoes	Basil, lavender, mint, rosemary
Moths	Lavender, sage, pennyroyal
Snails	Garlic, parsley, sage

| Thrips | Pyrethrum |
| Whitefly | Nasturtium, basil, marigold |

Essential oils make potent smelling sprays which will deter most self-respecting pests.

A multifaceted attack on snails and slugs

- Create barriers with smelly plants: *wilde als*, wormwood, southernwood, mint, chives, garlic, geranium, fennel, comfrey, lavender, rosemary and carnations.
- Sprinkle one or more of these around the plants: diatomaceous earth, finely crushed eggshells, grit, sand, crushed nutshell, seashell gravel, pine needles, oat bran (expands inside the pest), sawdust, hair, coffee and grounds.
- Trap them with the remains of cat and dog food, upside-down cabbage leaves, halved, empty citrus skins, an old carpet or beer.
- Rub grease or Vaseline around the rims of pot plants.
- Blend Yucca leaves with water, strain and spray. A vinegar and water spray is also effective.
- If you dare, copper wire around affected plants gives snails an electric shock, so they just keep away.
- Make a bait of two teaspoons of iron sulphate in two litres of water and pour it over some oats. Place the mixture in a shallow plastic container and put it among your plants. It completely takes away their appetite and kills them by absorbing water from their slime-making glands.

Never give up! Try one or all.
If all these fail, get yourself a duck …

CHAPTER TEN
Food from trees

Our indigenous trees are a good source of food: they're both beautiful and bountiful. Their fruits are very rich in vitamin C, which is partly what makes them so acidic. Often they are also rich in protein, fat, carbohydrates or minerals. But if you don't want to plant "wild" trees, you can choose from many other trees that produce food in your garden.

In the media, and whenever concerned citizens of Planet Earth come together, they continually talk about global warming and climate change. And so they should. Yet, although they could make a lasting and positive impact on these disturbing trends, too few people seem to want to change their lifestyles even a smidgen. It doesn't have to be a drastic, life-altering change. It can be as simple and rewarding as planting one or two trees.

- Trees benefit the total life-giving sytems (or **ecosystems**) of the world.

- They provide proper places to live (or **habitats**) for many creatures that play significant roles in maintaining the balance of nature.

- Trees fertilise and look after the soils.

- They absorb massive quantities of carbon dioxide and release life-giving oxygen.

- They absorb the falling rain and slowly release it back into the atmosphere or into the groundwater supplies.

- They provide the magic, medicine and poison that minister to the mind and spirit of man.

- They provide fuel, timber, shade and shelter.

- Last but not least of all, they provide food for the physical body. This is, perhaps, more important in the minds of many people.

Indigenous trees are a source of all these things.

Over hundreds of years the wild trees in this country have provided sustenance – the difference between hunger and plenty, life and death – for people and their livestock and for the wild animals which they hunted and on which they fed.

Today, with our so-called sophisticated tastes, many of these tree foods are unappealing to the palate. But don't be put off planting them. They are perfectly adapted to local conditions and provide food for the local wildlife, which is an integral part of a healthy garden system.

With this in mind, start planting trees. Create your own forest – your own lungs – providing food, shade, security, dust traps, windbreaks, habitats and much more. Invite life back into your landscape.

When we plant trees, we plant the seeds of peace and seeds of hope. We also secure the future for our children ...
WANGARI MAATHAI
(KENYAN WINNER OF THE NOBEL PEACE PRIZE)

Choosing the right tree

Whatever your choice of trees, the principles behind planting and maintaining them are the same.

Here are a few points to consider before you start:

- Trees take far longer to grow than any other garden features, so they should be planted first.
- Choose trees that serve more than one purpose. For example, the Natal plum (*Carissa macrocarpa*) provides wind protection, security (with its vicious thorns, it is much better than electric fencing), vitamin C and pectin. Rich fruits for you and the wild birds to eat. Its dense growth provides a place of refuge for an assortment of creatures. The Kei apple (*Dovyalis caffra*) has the same attributes. Both make excellent boundary plants.
- Consider the height to which each tree will grow and consider the spread of their different canopies. Trees will compete with plants growing near them for water and for soil nutrients. They may also cast shadows, which could be a problem, particularly if the shade blocks out the morning sun.
- Do not plant vigorous growers near your house. You will definitely live to regret it when the spreading and bulging roots cause your walls to crack and your drains to become blocked. Tree felling and repairs then become very expensive.
- The best time to plant is at the beginning of the rainy season, either in autumn or spring, depending on where you live. Not only will the rain boost the growth of the trees, but the newly-planted trees will receive much less stress from the dehydrating effect of the boiling sun.
- Smaller, or younger, trees are better able to survive the shock of being transplanted. Large trees are not only expensive to buy but will have large root systems confined in small containers and will therefore be root bound. They also need far more water to establish themselves.

How to go about planting a tree

Start by digging a large, square planting hole: at least half a metre by half a metre and half a metre deep. The larger the better so, if you're up to it, try make it one metre cubed.

Break up the subsoil at the bottom of the hole and work in plenty of organic matter: dry grass, straw, manure and partially decomposed compost.

If you have no objections to using animal products in your soil, add a few generous handfuls of bone meal.

Fill the hole by adding an 8 cm (four-finger) layer of subsoil followed by a 2 cm layer (one finger) of compost or well-rotted kraal manure, kitchen waste or dry grass.

Water these two layers well and continue adding layers of soil (first the subsoil and then the topsoil) and compost until all the soil has been replaced. The surface of the filled hole will be higher than the surrounding ground.

NOTE: When you add organic matter and water each level in turn, you will create a sponge effect. This will hold the water below the surface and so encourage the tree's roots to grow downwards, giving them greater strength. Surface watering tends to make plant roots stay near the surface.

Scoop the soil from the centre of the circle to the outside to create a basin effect.

Mulch the surface of the basin and plant seeds or seedlings on the inside of the ridge, in circles. It is extremely important to keep the beds well mulched as this prevents water loss by evaporation.

Plant your young tree in the centre of this basin. Firm it in well, and water.

Stake the tree with a simple post, which you will need to anchor standing straight up, as close to the trunk as possible.

Now tie the young tree to the post with a piece of nylon stocking or plastic so that it is held fairly firmly but can still move a little with the wind.

NOTE: Evidence suggests that movement of the trunk in the wind strengthens its base and leads to a stronger root system. After all, that is what happens in nature. Avoid using things like wire because it has no "give" and will cut into the trunk as the tree grows.

If you want to keep the sponge effect going, plant a one-metre piece of plastic piping vertically next to the tree, with the top above the ground level. You can also use a large plastic bottle (first burn small holes into the bottom with a hot needle) or a tin can with holes in the bottom. Pour water into the open hole above ground so that the water is sunk deeply into the soil.

Last, but not least, mulch the surface of the hole to prevent the evaporation of water.

The following works well on a short slope. Dig a pit about 50 cm deep and 30 to 40 cm wide and fill it with a little manure and garden and kitchen waste. The pit collects run-off water and any soil that is carried by the water. You can also channel grey water from the bathroom or kitchen into the pit. Surround the hole with small plants, like mint, close to the top of the slope, and bigger ones, such as a banana tree that likes a lot of water, further down the slope.

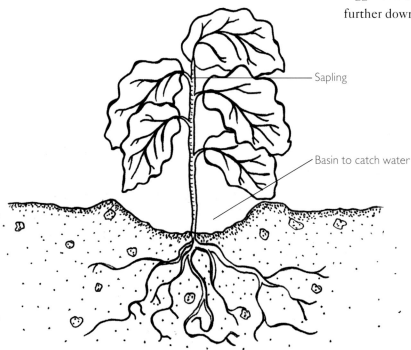

Sapling

Basin to catch water

Make a small depression around newly-planted trees. It will catch rain water and act as a reservoir.

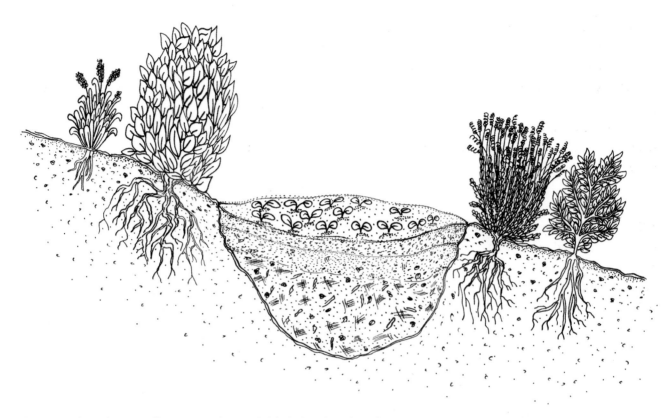

A planting pit catches run-off water on a slope and sinks it deep into the soil

Looking after your trees

- When the trees are young, deep watering is essential to encourage good root systems. Water the trees regularly until they are well-established.

- You will know soon enough if the roots are happy and growing because the top of the tree will also start growing. This is a sign that all is well and that your lavish attentions can be reduced somewhat.

- Give your tree a few handfuls of bone meal every spring and a good layer of compost or manure around its base in autumn.

- Remove dead and diseased wood and prune away overcrowded branches or those that are growing towards the centre of the tree. Also cut off any branches that grow up from the base.

- Established trees are well able to take care of themselves in terms of water and nutrients. That is what they have deep root systems for: searching for what they need in the depths of the soil.

Trees can also be grown from cuttings or truncheons. Refer to Chapter 12 for details.

Planting pits are a simple way of harvesting water for your plants.

Food trees for your garden

There is a list of food trees on page 26 which will help you in your research and decision-making. To give you a little indigenous inspiration, read on.

The Marula tree

Perhaps one of the best known wild fruits of Africa comes from the highly valued Marula tree (*Sclerocarya birrea*). It grows in the bushveld and woodlands, from KwaZulu-Natal through Swaziland and the northern parts of South Africa, to Botswana, Mozambique and Zimbabwe.

The Marula tree belongs to the same family (*Anacardiaceae*) as the mango, pistachio and cashew nuts, and also the pepper tree (*Schinus molle*), which is so common in the Karoo, where it offers weary travellers some respite from the heat at lay-bys along the Great North Road.

Marulas are deciduous trees, unable to tolerate frost. They seldom grow over 9 m and have spreading crowns with dense, graceful foliage. The delicate, spiky flowers are either male or female (occasionally a bisexual flower is produced) and are usually carried on separate trees. Only rarely do the male flowers produce a fruit. Insects flock to the flowering trees in summer, with their loud humming heard some distance away, giving one the feeling of noisy heat.

The fruits are fairly large, sweet-smelling, greenish-yellow berries, containing a large, hard seed. Inside each seed there are three nuts. In late summer, the berries ripen and fall to the ground where the strong scent attracts a plethora of wildlife. Reports of intoxicated elephants and baboons are not uncommon as over-ripe fruit ferments, giving off strong, turpentine-like smells.

As a food plant, the Marula is outstanding. The fleshy fruit is tart, thirst-quenching and energy-boosting. It's

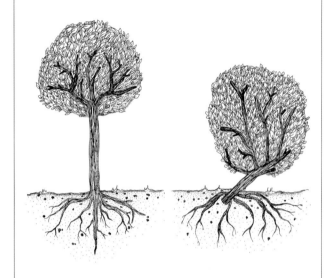

When you plant a tree from a seed, the way its stem and root system grow is different from that of a tree which you have planted from a cutting.

- Trees grown from seed have a tall stem and a deep tap-root system.
- Trees grown from a cutting often have a shorter stem (they bush close to the ground) and do not have a tap root.

very rich in vitamin C (reputedly four times higher than in a normal-sized orange) and, even when fermented, maintains a good vitamin C content. By the way, the juice is also claimed to be an aphrodisiac!

The nuts, incredibly difficult to extract from their shells, have a very high energy value, and contain roughly 30% protein and 60% fat and are an excellent source of nutrients. They are used by people in many ways. If you live in the right part of the world and you're lucky enough to have one of these trees in your backyard, here are a few recipes for you to try:

The wonderful Marula tree...

There is little wonder that the Marula tree is held in such high regard as every part of it is used in one way or another. Quite apart from its value as a food to humans, insects and game animals:

- The bark contains an anti-histamine, which soothes the blisters caused by hairy caterpillars.
- The timber is fairly light and soft and is used for furniture, panelling, drums, divining bowls and dishes.
- It is used as a prophylactic, to cure malaria and eye disorders. It is also used in the practice of magic, right down to the use of the bark from a male or female tree to pre-determine the sex of the unborn child.
- The amaZulu and Batsonga call it "the marriage tree" and hold it important in fertility rites and for instilling in a baby girl soft feminine traits.

- The dense crown provides shelter, shade and food for wild animals and reduces the evaporation of water from holes in the tree trunk.
- The magnificent green lunar moth lays her eggs on the leaves; the caterpillar hatches out, eats and then pupates in large cocoons which are used traditionally, filled with small pebbles, as ankle rattles.
- Marula oil is used in face creams and other body products, including the Enchantrix range.
- The oil is reputed to be a good preservative. When drizzled onto fresh meat which is then dried and stored, it keeps the meat for up to a year.

The Marula tree has thus HUGE potential as a cultivated, multi-purpose crop.

Marula flowers

Marula Jelly

2 kg ripe Marula berries
Sugar (heated in oven)

- Halve the berries, press the pips out into a mixing bowl and squeeze the berries hard over a mixing bowl to extract juice.
- Cover the pips and juice with water and turn out into a saucepan (not aluminium).
- Boil for 15 minutes.
- Strain through a nylon sieve lined with damp muslin.
- Use 250 ml heated sugar to 250 ml stock.
- Heat at a low temperature and stir until sugar has melted.
- Increase temperature and boil for 20 minutes or until setting point is reached. You can test for this by doing the "wrinkle test". Put a blob of the hot juice onto the back of an ice cube tray. Push with your finger. If the blob wrinkles, it is ready.
- Spoon hot jelly into sterilised jars with screw tops, and seal.

This jelly is best served with a rich venison pie or stew.

Marula Juice

5 kg ripe Marula berries
Sugar

- Pierce the berries so that the juice can escape and place in a saucepan. Cover with water and simmer for 20 minutes.
- Strain through a muslin cloth. Don't stir.
- Add 7 cups of sugar for every 10 cups of extract . Add lemon juice to taste.
- Bottle whilst still hot, in sterilised hot bottles.
- Date the bottles and store in a cool, dark place. Serve with ice in summer.

And then there are some interesting traditional African recipes, gleaned from Felicia Chiloane and Jackson Phala's *The Evaluation of the Marula Project* in Bushbuckridge in Limpopo Province:

Xigugu

• Put biltong (dried meat) and marula kernels in a mortar.

• Stamp until it is well mixed.

• Remove the mixture and place it in a bowl.

• Pour a spoon of marula oil over the mixture and serve.

Lekoma

• Braai maize meal until it is brownish in colour.

• Put maize meal into a mortar.

• Add marula kernels and a bit of salt and sugar.

• Then stamp all the ingredients until well mixed and serve.

Morogo (edible herbs)

• Cook morogo until ready.

• Crush marula kernels with a mortar and pestle.

• Add the crushed kernels to the morogo.

• Cook for about 10–20 minutes until it is whitish in colour.

• Keep on stirring the mixture.

• Take it off the fire and serve.

Dikokoro

• Cook fresh mealie grains until they are well cooked.

• Add full marula kernels into the pot.

• Cook for a few minutes and serve.

Last, but not least, you could always brew your own beer.

The waterberry *(waterbessie)* tree

Waterberry fruits

A tree that is frequently used by local councils for planting on pavements is the waterberry – also known as *waterbessie* (Afrikaans), *umdoni* (isiXhosa and isiZulu), *montlho* (Sepedi) and, more technically in Latin, *Syzigium cordatum*. Its beautiful, plum-coloured fruits are sought after by children and adults alike. They grow in profusion on these rather splendid trees.

The waterberry tree belongs to the family *Myrtaceae* along with the various guavas, pomegranates and Australian gums. Most people are also familiar with the common *Eugenia*, used as a hedging plant. We've all used allspice and cloves in the kitchen. These are the aromatic fruits and flower buds respectively of other members of this same family, with great commercial value in Asia.

An evergreen, water-loving tree, the waterberry occurs fairly widely in South Africa and in a wide range of habitats: ranging across forest margins, along water courses, in open bush and rocky outcrops and from sea level to altitudes of 1 600 metres. It reaches heights of 12 to 18 metres, the larger specimens being found in swamp forests, where they have been described as being "literally supported on top of quagmires by the tremendous spread of their roots".

Waterberries are dense, with round or spreading canopies, and are often more luxuriant at the coast where the air is more humid and water tables may be higher. In fact, it is believed that the presence of these trees in the wild indicates the presence of ground water.

The blue-green leaves are thick and leathery, well able to tolerate the gale-force winds in the south-western Cape and new foliage is bright red, which adds to the aesthetic appeal of the tree. In the wild, browsing animals such as the kudu eat the leaves and there are certainly birds such as the Crowned Hornbill which indirectly benefit by feeding off the hairy caterpillars of moths and butterflies that infest it occasionally.

In early spring and summer, the clusters of sturdy buds at the ends of the branches burst into creamy-white or pink flowers, which drop their petals very quickly, leaving little puffs of stamens. The flowers have a delicate scent, produce large amounts of nectar and provide a good food source for bees and other insects.

In late summer and autumn, the fleshy, deep-pink to purple berries ripen, each one with one pip, and these provide food for humans and a variety of animals including monkeys, birds, tortoises and mice.

This tree is perhaps one of the most useful in our arboreal pantheon:

- It provides nesting sites and habitats for a variety of wild life.

- Its bark provides a reddish-brown or orange dye.

- It is used as an emetic and to treat stomach complaints and diarrhoea.

- Its powdered bark is also used as a fish poison.

- The leaves and roots are used for treating respiratory ailments and tuberculosis.

- The timber is heavy and hard, strong and elastic, with a beautiful grain and, after seasoning in water, has been used for beams and rafters, furniture, boat building and fuel.

- It is purportedly strongly fire-resistant. Perhaps we should be planting more of it as fire-breaks in vulnerable areas.

- The berries are a source of purple dye, food for humans and animals, and are used for making alcoholic drinks and flavoured vinegars. Indeed, with a stretch of the imagination and a sense of adventure, a bowl of deep purple waterberries with their sweet-sour taste with just a hint of green apple could be quite a novel addition to your culinary experience.

By the way, please don't confuse our waterberries with the American term for small watermelons, or a cocktail combination of watermelon and strawberries!

Here are a few novel ideas for incorporating these berries into both sweet and savoury dishes.

Before you start, there are three points to keep in mind:

- You will need a lot of waterberries to make a small portion of jam or sauce, simply because they have a very high water content.

- Take care to pick only the ripest berries so that the bitter-tasting stalks are not included in the food.

- You will have to remove the pits before using them. Luckily, this is very easy.

- They have a very delicate flavour so it is best not to combine them with other strong flavours.

Leaves of the waterberry

Waterberry and Mint Sorbet

(Makes about 600 ml)

250 ml water

250 ml white sugar

1 litre waterberries (pitted)

1 teaspoon mint jelly

1 egg white

- Chop waterberries finely in a food processor.
- Add the chopped berries to a saucepan with water, 200 ml of the sugar and mint jelly.
- Heat gently and stir until the sugar has dissolved.
- Remove from the heat and let the mixture cool.
- Place mixture into ice-cream machine and let it churn. As soon as the mixture starts to freeze, remove.
- Whisk the egg white until stiff, add 50ml sugar and continue beating until it is smooth and shiny (the meringue stage) and fold into sorbet mixture.
- Put the mixture into a container and freeze.

NOTE: If an ice-cream machine is not available, place the mixture into the freezer and break the forming ice crystals every hour with a whisk.

Waterberry Compote

(Makes 250 ml)

300 g waterberries (pitted)

100 g sugar

1 small cinnamon stick

2 star anise

Water to cover

- Place the ingredients in a saucepan and bring to boil.
- Turn down the heat and cook until thickened. The mixture must coat the back of a spoon when hot.
- Remove from the heat and let cool.
- The mixture will thicken when cold and has a slight jammy consistency.

You can also try steeping them in cider vinegar for a richly coloured, flavourful vinegar or making jam and cordials. Try plucking them off the tree as you take a leisurely walk through your garden in the evening. They will most certainly boost your immune system and provide you with the purple pigments necessary for good health.

Easy to cultivate, hardy and fast-growing, attractive and a dense shade tree, the waterberry is a worthwhile addition to any garden. You can even grow your own specimen from seed which should be planted as soon as it is ripe, and before it dries out.

The Kei apple

Vicious spines of the Kei apple make it a good choice as a fencing plant

During the previous autumn in Cape Town when I wrote this book, a bountiful crop of roundish, velvety, bright-yellow fruits, with thick succulent flesh, carpeted the ground beneath a tree in the grounds of a hospital on the Cape Flats. Unusual in that part of the world, the Kei-apple tree had done itself proud, yet people had not discovered this rich source of food on their doorstep. What the birds did not eat simply fell to the ground to ferment, attracted fruit flies, and rotted away, returning all of its remaining nutrients to the soil.

The tree, a Kei apple, *Dovyalis caffra*, is well known all over the eastern parts of the country, common in open bush and wooded grassland, and often near termite mounds. It belongs to a cosmopolitan family, *Flacourtiaceae*, which are all good, fruit-bearing shrubs or trees, very often armed with vicious spines, and its name derives from the Kei River where it grows in abundance as a thick, shiny, spiny shrub, up to 3 metres in height. The branches are armed with straight, robust spines up

to 7 centimetres long. Some trees may grow to 9 metres with a thick crown of green foliage; these large specimens are often less spiny, as the tree has put its energy into its bulk, rather than into thorn production.

The tree is known by a variety of other names: Dingane's apricot, wild apricot, *wilde-appelkoos*, *appelkoosdoring* (Afrikaans), *umqokolo* (isiXhosa and isiZulu), among others. Although it is indigenous to warmer areas, it will survive mild frost, and long periods of drought. It even grows well in poor soils.

The Kei apple makes a worthwhile addition to your garden as it serves a multitude of purposes, not least of which is as a source of food for humans and animals alike. The fresh, ripe fruits are rich in vitamin C and pectin and, following the example of the Bapedi, who squeeze the juice onto their *pap*, they would make an excellent addition to a fruit salad and to muesli and yoghurt.

Nature seems to know best when to give us the right foods to boost our immune systems in preparation for the onslaught of winter colds and flu. In addition, Egyptian scientists have also reportedly identified 15 different amino acids (the building blocks of proteins) in the fruit. Monkeys and baboons, antelope and birds recognise their health-giving qualities and devour them voraciously in the wild!

Most people, however, consider the fruit too acid to eat out-of-hand, even when fully ripe. So, cut the fruits in half, remove the peel and the two rings of hairy seeds. Sprinkle with sugar and leave them to sit for a few hours before serving as a dessert or adding to a fruit salad. The fruits can be cooked but take only a few minutes of cooking before they turn into a sauce. Thicken this with a little crème fraiche and serve it over ice cream.

Kei apples are more usually made into delicious jams and jellies or, when unripe, into pickles.

Insignificant male and female flowers are borne on separate Kei-apple trees in late spring, giving rise to bunches of brightly coloured fruits on the female trees. Not only will this create a visual feast for you in the bleakness of autumn but will also attract a plethora of birds to the garden. Apart from their immediate appreciation of a food supply, the birds will take advantage of the thorny boughs in order to anchor their nests and to seek protection for their young from marauding cats and other predators.

Try planting a tree among shrubs in a mixed border designed to attract birds. Include such plants as the Bush-tick Berry (*Chrysanthemoides monilifera*), Puzzle Bush (*Ehretia rigida*), Mickey Mouse Bush (*Ochna serrulata*), Dune Crowberry (*Rhus crenata*), Cape Honeysuckle (*Tecomaria capensis*) and Lemon Pistol Bush (*Duvernoia aconitiflora*). Work out your planting plan to ensure a supply of food around the year.

In the Eastern Cape, barriers around kraals and sometimes fields are often made of the thorny branches of trees like the Kei apple. Urban gardeners can also take advantage of the ferocious barbs by planting the trees as a living fence, which will ultimately create an impregnable barrier. The plant has the habit of retaining its lower branches, unlike many other species, to create a good, thick hedge. No more catapulting over electric fences and razor wire. One landing in a Kei-apple tree will sort out the derrière of even the most earnest thief, while wire-cutters will make little impression on the woody boughs.

Cultivation from seed is easy. Allow the fruits to dry out, remove the seeds and sow them quickly before they lose their vitality. Interestingly, although this tree has no showy flowers, it is grown widely in other parts of Africa, Australia, the Mediterranean countries, and in England, where it is cultivated for its fruit or as a hedging plant.

Kei-apple Jam

Because of the apple's high level of acidity, no lemon juice needs to be added to the jam.

450 g Kei apples, halved, peeled, de-seeded and thinly sliced

450 g white sugar

Grated zest of one lemon (be careful not to include the bitter white pith)

1 teaspoon ground cinnamon (or 1 large stick)

1 tablespoon raisins, a bay leaf, 2 cloves – optional extras

- Pack the sliced fruit into a jar.
- Stand the jar of fruit in a saucepan of boiling water and let the apples stew for about 15 minutes or until they start to become tender.
- Put the Kei apples into a clean, heavy-bottomed pot.
- Add the sugar and the grated lemon zest.
- Simmer for 20 minutes, removing any scum as it rises to the surface.
- Add the cinnamon and any of the other optional extras.
- Place the jam into small sterilised jars with airtight lids.

The Kei-apple jam will keep for a long time in a cool, dry place.

The fruits of the Kei apple attract birds; the thorns deter thieves

Of course, no food garden should be without a lemon tree

Along with other citrus fruits, the lemon (*Citrus limon*) is one of the most widely consumed fruits in the world today. Apart from using the juice in all sorts of ways in the preparation of foods and cordials, lemon peels and the underlying white pith contain a number of health-giving substances. The lemon tree is perhaps one of the most valuable additions to the kitchen garden.

The first lemon trees to arrive at the Cape were imported from St Helena and planted in the Company's garden by Jan van Riebeeck. These were the predecessors of the rough-skinned lemon that we grow today and which is frequently used as a rootstock onto which other citrus varieties are grafted.

The lemon tree belongs to the family *Rutaceae*, which includes about 800 species, nearly all of which are characterised by oil glands on the leaves. Hold a lemon leaf up to the light and you will see tiny translucent dots. Interestingly, the various types of buchu (highly prized for their medicinal properties), the Cape Chestnut, White Ironwood, Horsewood and Knobwood, are all included in this family. By the way, the citrus family is not indigenous to South Africa and is thought to have originated in South East Asia and China.

We are all familiar with at least some of the uses of lemons in the kitchen and in the home:

- A drizzle of lemon juice over freshly cut fruits and vegetables stops the cut surfaces turning brown and unsightly in the presence of air.
- Lemon juice is a healthier addition to salad dressings, mayonnaise and marinades than vinegar as it has an alkalising effect on the blood.
- Lemon juice brings out flavours, adds tartness to titillate the taste buds and reduces the richness of meat and seafood dishes.
- Various drinks, iced teas, punches and the like would not be the same without a dash of lemon juice, or a sliver of the fruit.
- The acidity and the pectin contained in lemons are an integral part of the jam-making process.
- Lemon zest (peel) is used to flavour a variety of dishes (both sweet and savoury) and preserves. It is also laden with aromatic oils. Most of us have, at least once in our lives, squeezed the peel into the flame of a candle for a mini fireworks display.
- And, of course, lemon juice is a rich source of vitamin C and, therefore, an important part of the diet. Hot lemon and honey served up to cold and flu patients is soothing and healing.

Many of us are wondering why we are feeling tired, have aching joints, are overweight and suffer from candida. Doctors Robert Young and Shelly Redford explain in their book, *The pH Miracle*, the negative effects on one's metabolism of having acidic body fluids.

- We haven't mentioned the other uses of lemon juice as an astringent for the skin, as a bleach for nappies and perspiration stains, and an addition to furniture and brass polish. It removes urine smells, makes hair shine, removes mildew and black ink, and so the list goes on.
- There is a whole host of other medicinal benefits of the lemon. Those important phytochemicals have been shown to play a part in fighting cancer through their anti-oxidant properties; to prevent and repair damage to DNA; and to prevent the spreading of tumours.

- The white pith, below the zest, contains rutin which strengthens the walls of blood vessels and helps to prevent heart and circulatory problems.

It makes you think that having your very own lemon tree would be a very good idea and that a lemon a day would do a lot for your health and well-being.

Visit your local nursery once you have identified a protected spot in your garden. Lemon trees do not take kindly to strong, drying winds or frost, and prefer well-drained, light soils. There are a number of cultivars from which to choose:

- The Cape rough-skinned lemon is not very sour, the trees start bearing when very young and have fruit on them nearly all year round.
- Eureka is a vigorous tree which bears large juicy fruits with very few pips.
- Meyer trees also bear large fruit, but only one crop a year.
- Villa Franca is similar to Eureka but also bears only one crop a year.

An added benefit of having a lemon tree in your garden is that you will be visited by the magnificent Citrus Swallowtail butterfly (*Papillio demodocus demodocus*) which will not only feast on the nectar from the fragrant flowers, but also use the leaves as the nursery and feeding grounds for its young.

All great cooks use lemons.

Get out there and make a difference to your landscape and to your future. Research the trees, plant them, care for them, harvest the fruits of your labour and sit beneath them in your old age.

The Tree

Let us pause for the taking of inventory,
To measure the debt we owe the tree.
For the searching root that knits the soil,
The cooling shade for those who toil,
The air we breathe,
Nature's greatest gift,
And the leaf that heralds
Each season's shift.

Forget not the fruit
that feeds man and beast,
That branch that burns
 to prepare the feast.
That sturdy frame
that builds the home,
And the paper on which you read this poem.

The tree gives all
And asks no prize,
Even making the axe
That ends its life.
(ANONYMOUS)

Lemon Cordial

A deliciously refreshing drink served with water or soda.

Juice of 10 to 12 lemons

Grated rind of 3 to 4 lemons

2½ kg sugar

1 packet tartaric acid (15 ml or 1 tablespoon)

1 packet citric acid (15 ml or 1 tablespoon)

1 packet Epsom salts (15 ml or 1 tablespoon)

2 litres boiling water

• Dissolve the sugar, tartaric acid, citric acid and Epsom salts in the boiling water.

• Add the grated lemon rind and lemon juice.

• Mix together and allow to cool.

• Pour the cordial into sterilised glass or plastic bottles and store in a refrigerator.

• Dilute with water (or soda water) to taste.

• Add ice cubes and a sprig of mint for a refreshing summer drink or add boiling water and a slice of lemon for a winter drink.

Lemon Curd

The most delicious spread for hot toast, scones and muffins. It tastes so good that you can eat it by the spoonful straight out of the jar. Use other citrus fruit or granadillas to make a change.

100 g butter

200 g sugar

4 eggs

Juice and grated rind of 4 lemons, or 3 oranges and 1 lemon, or 2 lemons and the pulp of 4 granadillas

• Melt butter and sugar in double boiler.

• Add well-beaten eggs and juice and rind of lemons (and/or oranges or granadilla pulp).

• Continue heating, stirring occasionally until the mixture has thickened like custard.

• Pour into clean, heated jam jars.

• Seal and store in a cool cupboard, or refrigerate.

• Eat within a month.

(Freezes well)

CHAPTER ELEVEN

Gardening in containers

If space is an issue, there are many ways to get around it…

If you have a patio, a balcony, an open stairwell or a flat roof (in fact, if you hardly have any space at all), you can still become a productive, part-time container "farmer". Remember that all that plants need to grow is plenty of sunshine; water; fresh, circulating air; and something to root in that will provide the nutrients they need.

Preparing your containers

Boxes, baskets, used tyres, plastic bags and bottles, buckets, tins, basins and baths – anything that will hold soil – are some of the containers you can use to grow crops for food or profit. Clay pots and wooden boxes make excellent containers because they are porous and can "breathe" through the sides, creating good air circulation for the roots. But they also absorb water from the soil mix, causing it to dry out rapidly. So, if you grow plants in porous containers, you will need to water them more frequently.

You may find it necessary to line the containers you have with plastic in order to keep the moisture in, or with cardboard and newspaper in order to hold the soil.

Make sure that there are adequate drainage holes in the bottom of the container in order to allow excess water to escape. Water-logged pots reduce the amount of air around the roots and this results in disease and death.

Recycle your tyres for containers

Tyres are ideal as containers for plants. You can layer them one, two or three deep in whatever arrangement suits your site.

- A thick layer of newspaper or cardboard underneath the bottom tyre will stop the grass from growing into it.
- On a verandah, you may first want to put a sheet of heavy plastic underneath the bottom tyre to prevent stains. You might want to move the container later on.
- Fill the bottom layer of tyres with a good potting mix (equal parts compost and good garden soil, and a handful of wood ash).
- Pack the soil well into the side walls before filling the centre.
- Smooth and level the soil and you're ready to plant – either seeds or seedlings.
- The depth of your tyre construction will determine what you plant.
- Also remember that it is a good idea to plant cut-'n'-come-again crops such as beans, spinach, tomatoes, and green peppers because they will give you a supply of food over a long period without your having to keep replanting.
- Don't forget to cover the soil with mulch to conserve water, feed the soil, prevent weed growth and control temperature.
- Cucumbers and climbing beans need trellises for support; these can be erected using old broomsticks and odd pieces of wood.
- Stop any cats from peeing in the pot plants by arranging used plastic forks and knives menacingly around the base of the plants.

Make up a rich potting mix, using one part garden loam and one part good-quality compost. A few handfuls of coarse grit will ensure a better draining mix.

If you don't have any compost available, you can make your own by chucking your own waste into a basket or a wooden box, or even into a small hole in the ground. You can use household waste (such as vegetable scraps, crushed egg shells, shredded newspapers, corn cobs and husks), garden waste (such as oak leaves, weeds or grass clippings), vegetable waste from a local market or restaurant, animal dung and sawdust.

Keep the mixture moist, throw in a few handfuls of soil to introduce lots of microbes and stir it every few days to speed up the rotting process.

After several weeks, you will have a compost mix that will really improve your soil.

Start to fill your containers by first covering the drainage holes with pebbles, corks or pieces of broken pots and then cover these with a bit of gravel and a piece of old sacking (made of natural fibre). This will prevent the potting mix from clogging the holes.

Now add your soil and compost, filling the containers to about 1 cm from the top. The soil will settle a little and the space this leaves at the top will allow for mulch and watering.

Looking after your container gardens

Make sure they get enough light. Container vegetables need the same amount of light as those growing in an open garden – at least six hours of full sun daily. Leafy greens and some root crops get by with less light but fruiting plants, like tomatoes and beans, need full sun.

Water frequently…

Soil in containers dries out more quickly than in the garden. Containers may need watering at least once a day, twice in warm, dry weather. Check daily. If the top 2 cm feel dry, water thoroughly till water runs out at the bottom. If your containers stand on a tray with an open end, the run-off water could be caught in a basin and used again.

Mulch the surface of the container with wood chips, pebbles or shredded leaves and dry grass.

Feed regularly…

Frequent watering leaches nutrients out of container soil, therefore feed frequently – at least once a week with dilute solutions of manure tea or compost tea. If you have an earthworm farm, the worm tea makes an excellent tonic.

How do you decide what to grow?

Choosing good container crops

Begin with your family's dinner plate. Grow what you need to add more nourishment and variety to your diet. Also think about what is expensive to buy, and hard to obtain.

Green leafy vegetables are a good bet; they grow quickly, give a good yield and are important in a healthy diet.

Beans of many kinds, herbs, peppers and tomatoes also do well in containers.

Grow what will give you a good return for your work for as much of the year as possible. Many of these plants are what we call cut-'n'-come-again plants. The more you pick, the more they produce.

Cabbages and cauliflowers provide a one-off harvest, take a long time to grow and take up a lot of space.

A raised tyre garden

Fruit trees and herbs also do well in containers.

Container gardening is important in cities where there is a shortage of space. Not only does it boost a family's nutrition, but the plants themselves recycle waste and clean the air, helping to make the city a better place for everyone.

And some added bonuses…

Container gardeners even find that their houses are cooler in summer and warmer in winter because the containers and plants protect their houses from extreme temperatures. It's also a good way to conserve water.

When you move home, you can take your food garden with you. Why not improve the life of your family and your neighbourhood by starting a container garden?

Sprouts are the easiest-to-grow, most power-packed, year-round food

*Start an organic sprout farm
and a "fast-food outlet"
on your kitchen windowsill.*

It will save you time, money and water.

They grow very quickly, are always fresh and are uncontaminated by pesticides. You can eat them everyday in salads, stir fries and sandwiches, in soups and stews, or just as a snack. They are the most economical food and use very little water to grow. The rinsing water can be used in your garden or added to the cooking pot.

Clive McCay, professor of nutrition at Cornell University, once described soya bean sprouts as an almost perfect food – "A vegetable which will grow in any climate, will rival meat in nutritive value, will mature in three to five days, may be planted any day of the year, will require neither soil nor sunshine, will rival tomatoes in vitamin C, will be free of waste in preparation and can be cooked with little fuel…" And cheap, into the bargain.

Some seeds from your kitchen cupboard that you can sprout:
Lentils, chickpeas, soya beans, peas, peanuts, mung beans, fenugreek, mustard and alfafa (lucerne). You can even sprout onion and broccoli seeds.

NOTE: Never eat the seeds from the packets that you buy for planting in your garden. They may have poison on them!

How to go about sprouting

- Place one tablespoon of seeds in a large, clean glass jar.
- Cover with water and leave to soak overnight.
- In the morning, drain off the water and tie a piece of mesh over the top of the jar (an old stocking or an orange mesh bag will do the job just fine).
- Rinse the seeds with clean water at least twice a day. You may need to put the bottle lid over the mesh covering to prevent the sprouting seeds from drying out in between rinsings.
- Keep the seeds in a warm, dark place until the tiny roots and shoots appear and then put them in a sunny place so that the baby leaves turn bright green.
- On the fourth day, depending on how warm the weather is, the sprouts should be ready to eat.

P.S. One tablespoon of alfafa seeds will give you about 250 g or more of sprouts. That's a lot of food!

Jam jars covered with orange mesh bags make perfect containers for growing sprouts

Sprouts are not all that you can grow on the kitchen windowsill…

Grow your own baby greens

Turnips, beetroots, radishes and carrots are usually grown for their roots but their leaves (especially young ones) are delicious and very nutritious.

Next time you harvest (or buy) any of these vegetables, cut off the crown, about half a centimetre from the top.

Eat the root, cooked or raw, and save the crown.

Stand the crowns in water in a shallow tray in a sunny place.

Water regularly and, within a week, the first new growth will start to show.

Pick the new, baby leaves when they are about 10 cm long and add them to a salad or a stir-fry, or sauté them in a little olive oil as a side-dish.

Carrot tops taste like a cross between coriander and parsley and make an unusual addition to your food.

And while we're looking at growing veggies in a rather unusual manner… try growing sunflower seeds, lentils and dhanya (coriander) in discarded polystyrene trays, cottage cheese containers or any other suitable discarded packaging.

Fill the trays to about a centimetre from the top with compost or good garden soil.

Sow the seeds so that the soil surface is pretty much covered (only one seed deep though).

Cover them over with a light sprinkling of soil, compost or vermiculite. You can even cover them with wet newspaper or kitchen towel but you will have to keep looking to see when the seeds are sprouting so that you can remove the cover and give them the light they need to grow.

Baby beet leaves growing from discarded crowns

Use a north-facing wall to create vertical gardens

You can build a simple construction of wooden planks and rope to hang up on a north-facing wall. This will provide vertical space for you to grow a variety of plants in order to add essential nutrients to your diet. Here are some examples of what you can grow:

- Two carrots in an old milk box or bag.
- A parsley plant in an old chamber pot.
- Chives and spring onions in a plant pot.

Water them lightly and make sure that the soil remains damp while they are germinating.

Keep in a warm, sunny place.

The young green shoots are ready to eat in about a week to ten days.

Snip them off with a pair of kitchen scissors and pop them into your salad, a sandwich or the juicer.

The lentils will re-grow a few times but one sunflower seed gives you one juicy sprout.

So often one sees bunches of wilted, very sad-looking dhanya (coriander) in the supermarkets. Growing your own, as described above, means having it crisp and fresh all the time and, like turnip and beet tops, dhanya is rich in vitamin A, which is so essential for boosting the immune system.

Wheat and barley greens are just as easy to produce. Since you do not a have a full set of grinding molars like true herbivores, however, you will need to put the young shoots through a juicer to extract the goodness.

What could be easier than creating a mini-garden in your kitchen?

Careful planning and succession planting will ensure that there is always something fresh and green to add to your meal.

Hanging gardens make good use of vertical space

- Dhanya seeds in a variety of shallow plastic trays. They will give you loads of seedlings, which you can snip off when you need them. Dhanya, by the way, has a very high vitamin A content and makes an interesting addition to meals.

Use your eyes and your imagination to design a novel container garden.

Use what you can find on your travels around your neighbourhood and the wider countryside.

This way, it costs you nothing and conforms to the spirit of using what we have, while adding nothing to the consumerist way of life.

Best of all, it triggers the flow of those creative juices that have probably been stagnating in the back of beyond.

Maybe you didn't even realise you had them.

Chapter Twelve

Growing your own plants from seeds and slips

This is a most rewarding exercise, and certainly a cost-effective one, if you follow some simple rules. You will first need to set yourself up with a few basic items:

- A protected place, or nursery: this could be a sheltered spot under a tree, or something that you build:

You will also need

- A supply of good compost and vermi-compost
- Coarse river sand
- Wood ash
- Newspaper and cardboard
- Plastic bottles
- Milk or fruit juice boxes
- Foil trays or pie dishes
- A wooden plank about 50 cm long and 10 cm wide
- A pencil, a ruler or a small wooden rod
- Something to write with – a laundry marker, an old ballpoint pen, a wax crayon
- Any other waste material that is useful for containers, labels, protection of seeds and seedlings. Just look around you for what you need.

Growing your own plants from seeds

A seed is a tiny part of a plant that can grow in the soil to produce a new plant. It contains an **embryo** (a little baby) plant and a store of food for the young plant to grow, once the seed germinates. Later on it will absorb nutrients from the soil and begin to trap sunlight energy, air and rain for further growth.

Germination

Germination takes place when the temperature is just right, enough water is present and the seed coat is soft enough. The seed soaks up enough water for the embryo inside to begin forming a seedling. This is the beginning of germination.

The tiny embryo plant gets the food that it needs to grow and develop from the seed leaves or **cotyledons**. It is only once the tiny true leaves are exposed to sunlight that they are able to start making food for the further growth and development of the little plant.

It is important to understand what happens when seeds germinate because many people who try and grow their own plants from seed are not successful. In fact, many new gardeners tell us that they do not want to grow from seed because there are too many problems ... it takes too long and it is more work for them.

It is a good idea to grow your own plants from seed for a number of reasons …

- It is far cheaper than purchasing seedlings from a nursery or garden shop. A packet of seeds may contain over 300 seeds – many more depending on the type of plant. Assuming that all the seeds germinate, work out the cost of each seedling by dividing the cost of the packet by the number of seeds. You'll possibly have to sit and count the seeds before you start but that saves you having to watch television. Then have a look at the cost of a tray of seedlings at your nearest nursery and calculate the cost of one seedling. Yes, it is definitely a matter of economics!

- If you grow your own, you can be sure that the seedlings are not root-bound and over their sell-by date when you transplant them into your garden. This will increase your chances of healthy plants and a bountiful harvest. You will also have peace of mind, knowing that your plants have not been treated with anything untoward.

- You can choose from an enormous variety of seeds. Ask for seed catalogues and go through them with a fine-tooth comb. They will really inspire you to "go gardening" and to try all sorts of combinations to suit your palate and your aesthetics.

See what other reasons you can come up with. There have to be good reasons to go the longer, and perhaps, more trying route.

Starting from seed sometimes means that you need to …

- have special equipment
- plan ahead
- have a cool, dry place to store the seed before you plant it
- store seed properly

Seeds need moisture and heat to germinate. Therefore, the best place to store seed is in a cool, dry place. You can keep them, for example, in a sealed glass jar in the fridge, where most flower and vegetable seeds can be kept for about two years; or in a dark, dry cupboard.

After sowing some of the seed out of a packet, always close it immediately and seal with a paperclip or an elastic band.

Do not store seeds in airtight containers, unless you deep-freeze them. Seeds are alive and they need air.

There are many things that need to be done before you can successfully sow seed. Read the following pages carefully, make a checklist and get everything ready *before* you open the seed packets.

Before you sow the seed, make sure that it is alive seed and will germinate and grow. You do not want to waste growing time by planting seed that will not germinate because it is too old and no longer viable.

To make sure that your seed is fresh …

- Put 50 seeds on a piece of damp cloth or paper towel into a plastic bag.
- Blow air into the bag and seal the end with an elastic band or a piece of string.
- Periodically blow into the bag so that mould does not develop.
- After about ten to fourteen days, check to see how many of the seeds have germinated.

Do a simple calculation….

If 40 seeds have germinated out of the original 50, the germination rate is 80%.

If fewer than 20 seeds have germinated (40% germination), then the seed is old and either you throw it away and buy fresh seed, or you will need to plant many more seeds than normal since there will be a low germination rate.

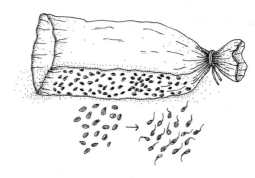

Check seed viability before planting

Suitable containers or seed trays

Anything will do as a seed tray as long as:

- It is at least 5 cm deep.
- It has drainage holes at the bottom.
- It is strong enough so that it doesn't lose its shape when you move it.
- It is not too heavy to move.
- It is not too small, because it will dry out too quickly.

Some ideas for seed trays …
Cleaning and sterilising seed trays

Scrub them well to remove all loose dirt and then pour boiling water over them.

or

Mix 40 ml of Jeyes fluid in 10 litres of water. Soak the containers in this mixture for one hour. Allow them to dry out in the sun before using them.

or

Make a herb tea out of sage and thyme, wild rosemary, *wilde als*, *khakibos* or rue. Fill a pot with a mixture of these herbs, cover with water and bring to the boil for 30 minutes. Mix in a little grated kitchen soap and use this to sterilise the seed trays.

Making a good soil mix for the seedling trays

It is important to make a rich mixture, so that the seedlings grow big and strong enough for planting out into the ground.

One measure well-rotted compost + one measure coarse river sand + one measure vermi-compost

> **or**

One measure well-rotted compost + one measure good garden soil + one measure coarse river sand

> **or**

Two measures well-rotted compost + two measures coarse river sand + 1/10 measure wood ash

- **Compost** absorbs and holds moisture. Use your own home-made compost as it is much cheaper.
- **Sand** gives drainage and prevents a hard crust forming on the surface. Replace the river sand with garden soil, if you do not have any river sand.
- **Wood ash** is not essential but it does help to sweeten the soil. **Never** use ash from coal, charcoal, anthracite or briquettes and make sure that no plastic has been burnt in the fire.
- **Vermi-compost** contains all the nutrients that the seedlings need and is rich in water-retaining humus.

Make sure that the soil mix
is free of weed seeds, "pesty" eggs,
and disease spores...

Pour boiling water over the filled seed trays, soaking them well, before sowing the seed. Make sure that the trays are on a level surface and that the water runs straight out of the bottom. Boiling water kills weed seeds, insect larvae and eggs, snail and slug eggs and bacterial and fungal spores.

Place the soil mix in a drum, with a grid placed about 30 cm from the bottom. The grid keeps the soil separate from the water underneath it. Heat the water over a fire. The heat of the water and steam will kill any weed seeds and disease organisms.

Filling the seed trays and sowing the seeds

Fill the seed tray with the soil mixture to within one to two centimetres from the top.

Firm the soil mixture down with a piece of wood or the palm of your hand. Make sure that it is level or the seeds will wash down into a corner when you water them.

Mark off rows about 5 cm apart with a piece of wooden rod, a ruler or a pencil, pressing it about half a centimetre into the surface.

Place the seeds into these furrows and cover with sifted soil or sand, to a depth about three to four times their width, depending on whether they are cool- or warm-weather crops.

Small seeds should not be buried but pressed into the soil instead.

Firm the soil down so that the seeds are in good contact with it.

Water the seed tray with a fine spray, being very careful not to wash the seeds out of the soil mix. Another good method is to soak the bottom of the container in a dish of water or to stand it on wet cardboard or newspaper, so that moisture is drawn up into the soil mix.

REMEMBER that the soil must be kept moist
at all times, but not soaking wet.

Label the tray with what you have sown and the date.

Put a piece of wet newspaper or sacking over the surface to keep the soil mix damp. You can also cover the seed tray with a sheet of clear plastic to retain moisture.

Place the seed tray in a warm, shady spot and do not let it dry out.

Watch for the first signs of germination.

The seeds will not need light until they have sprouted but they will need fresh air to prevent mould and fungus from growing.

Lift the cover for an hour or so each day to let fresh air reach the soil surface.

As soon as the seedlings first appear, remove the cover and make sure that the seed tray is in a cool place where it will receive good light (not direct sunlight which can burn the seedlings) and will be protected from wind.

Making labels for the seed trays

Some tips for successful germination

Seeds must have **warmth**, **moisture** and **air** to germinate.

Nearly all plants have a particular growing period. It is no use sowing summer plants, which need warm, bright growing conditions, in cold winter weather and vice versa. Check the seed-sowing chart for your area to find out what you can plant in any particular month of the year.

To speed up the rate of germination, soak large seeds in water overnight.

Do not plant seeds too shallow or too deep.

Remember the rule of thumb …
In cool weather, plant each seed deep enough
so that three or more of the same kind of seed
could lie on top of it. In hot weather, plant the seed deep
enough so that four more seeds of the same
kind could lie on top of it.

Mix very small seeds with dry river sand and trickle them along the furrows. Don't cover them at all – simply press them into the soil mix.

Some plants do not like to be transplanted

There are a number of plants that do not like to be transplanted and they need to be planted *directly* into prepared garden beds. Examples of these are beans, peas, broad beans, pumpkins, squash and marrows.

Once the seeds have germinated

If you have planted in polystyrene seed trays with plugs, you will not need to transplant the seedlings until they are about 10 cm tall and ready to go directly into the ground. If more than one seedling has come up in every plug, simply cut off the weaker one at ground level to give the remaining seedling a chance to grow strong.

If you have grown in furrows in seed trays, you will need to thin out the seedlings so that they will have a better chance to develop. As soon as the seedlings have grown a second pair of leaves, they are ready to be thinned. The second pair of leaves are usually their first true leaves, which are quite different from the seed leaves. They will still be very little – only about 3 cm or so tall – and their root systems will also be very small.

By this time, the seedlings have used up the food stored in the seed and will now need a lot of feeding.

Water the seed tray well before you start. Prepare a richer soil mix, which has good drainage and a loose texture, and fill the new containers.

Make holes with your finger (about 3 cm apart) in the soil mix in the new container ready for the transplanted seedlings.

Carefully prick out the seedlings, one at a time, and put them into the prepared holes. Use a small pointed stick or a triangular piece of hard plastic, without pulling on the stem or disturbing the roots or the other seedlings.

Push the soil around the roots so that they are planted at the same depth as they were before, and press them in firmly. Water well.

Looking after the seedlings

- Keep them in a cool, bright and airy place.
- Protect them from strong wind and direct sunlight.
- Keep them damp but not too wet.
- Give them regular doses of liquid fertilisers.
- As a part of your daily routine, watch out for insects, weeds and diseases.

A common disease in nursery plants is called "damping off". Plants get this disease if there is too much water in the seed bed and conditions are too hot. It is caused by a fungus which grows at the surface of the soil and causes the base of the stems to rot.

To prevent damping off, do not leave mulch on the bed or in the seed tray for a long time after the seeds have germinated. Also avoid overcrowding.

Frequent thinning, weeding and water control will prevent this disease from damaging your plants.

Planting out

After several weeks, when the seedlings are at least 10 cm tall, have four or more true leaves and their leaves are touching those of their neighbours, they are ready to be planted into the garden or into their permanent home.

Put the seedling tray in a shady place outside the nursery for a few hours each day before you plan to transplant. This helps the seedlings to adjust to the change from the protected nursery to the outdoors.

The day before planting, put them near the spot where you intend to plant them.

Any transplanting is a shock to the plant, so it must be done carefully and in the late afternoon or on a rainy or cloudy day (not in the mornings or in the midday heat).

Prepare your planting holes using a dibber and water them well.

Water the seedlings well and then loosen with a small fork, taking care not to damage them and keeping as much soil as possible around the roots.

Do not pick up the seedlings by the stems. Handle them by their leaves.

Plant the seedlings deeper than they were, right up to the first pair of leaves. This will help them to stand up and will encourage the formation of extra roots.

Firm the soil around the plant with your fingers, and water gently.

Protect the plant with some mulch drawn up to it but not touching the plant. Put a deep layer of mulch between the plants but do not cover them.

Make a shade hat for the plant out of an old milk carton. Leave the hat on for two to three days, until the plant has recovered.

If you have transplanted many seedlings into one bed, it is best to make a shade net out of shade cloth or vegetable bags sewn together, and to cover the whole bed.

There are many ways of growing your own plants other than from seeds …

Growing your own plants from cuttings or slips

To prepare or plant the cuttings

The cuttings should be about 10 cm long (about the distance from the tip of your index finger to the knuckle) and the thickness of a pencil. They can be taken by using a sharp knife or a pair of secateurs. Cut just below the node (where the leaves grow from the stem) or by taking a heel cutting at the node.

Carefully remove the lower leaves, allowing two or three pairs to remain at the top of the cutting.

Prepare the soil mix as described below for soft- and hardwood cuttings and place it in suitable containers with drainage holes at the bottom.

Make a hole in the soil mix with a pencil or a stick and gently push the cutting into it.

Plant so that two-thirds of the cutting is under ground and one-third is above the surface.

Push the soil firmly around the cutting and water it well.

To protect the cuttings from drying out, either put the cut-off top of a plastic cool-drink bottle over them, or make a mini hothouse using the underwires from an old bra. Tie clear plastic over these. The underwires create a

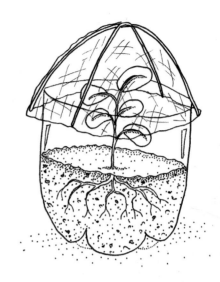

Mini hothouse

mini cloche and keep the plastic off the cutting, creating a humid environment around it.

Put the containers in a protected place but not in direct sunlight.

Keep an eye on them. You'll know when they've rooted because there will be signs of growth at the top of the cutting.

Cuttings may be taken from soft- or hardwood.

Softwood cuttings

Prepare the potting mix for softwood cuttings by mixing river sand, which allows good drainage, and a bit of vermiculite, which helps to retain some moisture. These can often be rooted in a container of water.

It is best to take cuttings from the tips of softwood stems and to remove most of the lower leaves.

The ones remaining at the top of the slip should be cut back to at least half their size or folded over. This reduces the amount of water lost through the leaves by evaporation but still allows the cutting to breathe. It also helps it to put its energy into developing roots and not into photosynthesising.

Do not remove the leaves entirely as some food energy is required to make food, although often these leaves will die and fall off. Don't despair if this happens. There should be enough chlorophyll in the green stem to tide the cutting over.

Some softwood plants drip sap after you have cut them. Let the cut ends dry before placing in the soil mix.

The best time to take softwood cuttings is in spring.

Remember: "S" for "Softwood" and "in Spring"

> Basil cuttings root very easily in a jar of water. Once rooted, pop into the soil.
>
> Experiment with New Zealand spinach, carnations and anything else in your garden, plus what you can glean from friends' gardens.
>
> Cuttings take a lot less time than seed to 'bear fruit'.

Hardwood or semi-hardwood cuttings

Remember: "W" for "Woody" and "in Winter"

It is best to take hardwood cuttings in winter, although you may take them in summer after there has been some new growth.

You can take these cuttings from woody herbs, fruit trees and grapevines, for example. The soil mixes for these two types of cuttings differ a little.

For semi-hardwood cuttings, make a mixture of river sand, a good soil mix (ideally loam), a bit of vermiculite and some compost. Don't be tempted to put in too much of the compost as it may cause the cuttings to rot before they root.

Hardwood cuttings will root in much the same as above but you can increase the amount of compost that you use.

A few words of caution …

Warm, moist conditions are ideal for your cuttings, but they will also promote the rapid growth of pests and diseases, so you will have to take extra care with hygiene, and be vigilant.

A few rules to establish for your propagating area are:

- Avoid using material from unhealthy or diseased plants.
- Keep your nursery, all work surfaces and your tools spotlessly clean.
- Keep cuttings away from soil and do not bring soil onto the surface where you are working. Soil, remember, is teeming with microbes and not all of them will be "good guys".
- Sterilise your soil mixes if you have any doubts about their hygiene.
- Remove any dead or dying material immediately and dispose of it outside the propagating area.

Taking care of your cuttings

All cuttings should be kept damp. This may mean watering twice a day – in the morning and afternoon – but check to see if they are still damp before watering a second time. It is very important not to over-water.

Once rooting has taken place, carefully remove each rooted slip and place into a slightly larger container, filled with a rich soil mix. Rooting may take a long time, especially for hardwood cuttings. As the new plant grows and fills the container, you can either transplant it into a still larger one or plant it in your garden.

Give the transplants …

- some tender, loving care
- a dash of extra compost
- lots of water till they've settled in well

- protection from excessive wind and sun
- a weekly boost with a "tea" of your choice

Growing trees from truncheons

This is an easy way to establish trees in the spot where you want them to grow. The best time to do so is in winter. It's simply a case of taking a piece of a branch (about one metre long or more), putting it the right way up in the ground so that about two-thirds of it is buried and leaving it to get on with it.

Make sure that you allow the cut surfaces to dry out before you plant the truncheon. This effectively forms a "scab" which prevents the entry of bacteria and fungi that may cause diseases.

The top end of the truncheon should also be cut at an angle, so that water does not sit on it and cause rotting.

Try this with fig-tree truncheons.

Some other propagating exercises for you to try

Grow your own sweet potatoes …

Sweet potatoes are able to grow well in hot, dry weather and will even survive drought. A good crop for the future.

Buy a few healthy sweet-potato tubers from your local supermarket or greengrocer.

Fill a dark-coloured container with water.

Find the end that was once attached to the mother plant and rest the tuber with this end facing downwards on the rim of the container.

Place it on a sunny window ledge and wait for it first to root and then to send out long leafy vines.

Cut the vines (or the **runners**) into 30 cm lengths, making quite sure that you remember which is the top and bottom of each cutting.

Bury the runners in moist soil to at least half their length, firming each cutting in well to ensure good rooting.

An interesting fact to bear in mind is that if you plant the lower half of the runner horizontally, it will produce a higher yield and larger sweet potatoes than if you plant it vertically.

Hey presto! In about four to five months you will have a crop of the most delicious sweet potatoes, but you will also have an excellent ground cover and protection for your soil. You can eat the sweet potato leaves as well – full of vitamin A, among other things.

Another way of growing them is to plant the tubers directly into the garden in early spring. Cover them with about 5 cm soil and water lightly, increasing the amount as the shoots start to run across the surface. After about eight weeks you should have plenty of runners from which to take cuttings. Proceed as above.

Grow your own potatoes in tyres or bags

It's easy to propagate potatoes which, by the way, are swollen underground stems. Don't eat all the potatoes you harvest. Use some as "seed potatoes" for your next crop.

Paint the tyres in light colours to keep the soil cooler for the potatoes. Either way, you maximise the use of horizontal space in a small garden by going upwards, and increase the yield of ordinary potatoes. The more tyres you add as the potatoes grow, the more tubers are formed.

Grow your own pineapples

Cut off the leafy top of the next pineapple you buy, keeping a small portion of the crown attached. Put it on top of a good potting mix, water it and proceed in the same way as for cuttings. After a while it will develop into a pineapple plant.

Grow your own ginger

The ginger tubers you buy are actually swollen underground stems. Look at one carefully and you will notice rings around the tuber and there are large buds developing on the sides, next to some of the rings. The rings represent scale-like leaves, which are reduced to this status because they are underground, and the buds are what will grow into new aerial foliage once the time is right.

If you plant a tuber in a rich loamy mix and keep it warm and damp, you will soon have a ginger plant which will spread horizontally, giving you an abundance of fresh ginger.

Grow your own mint and strawberries

Both are exceedingly easy to propagate from stem runners which grow along the ground. Roots and new plants develop wherever a node arises. A node is the point on the stem from which leaves or side branches emerge.

Grow two leeks for the price of one

Simply cut off the root tip of the leek and plant it. Cover with a cut-off clear plastic bottle for a few days to keep it warm and damp. Soon you will notice it is starting to grow small green leaves and within two months you'll have a fine new leek to eat. Replanting a tip to produce a *third* leek doesn't work; it will either rot, or go straight to seed.

Gardening can be fun.

Get out there and experiment.

You have nothing to lose, and everything to gain.

Did you know that every time you buy a bunch of leeks, you are getting two bunches for the price of one?

Two leeks for the price of one

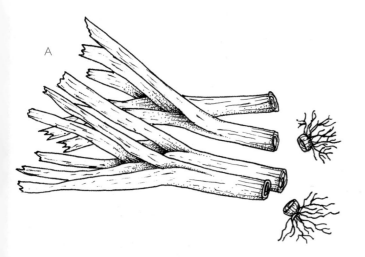

A

Cut the ends off the leeks

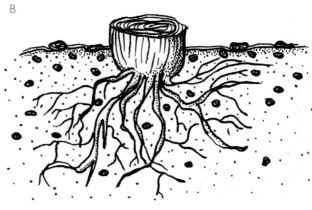

B

Plant the crown with its roots (trimmed if necessary)

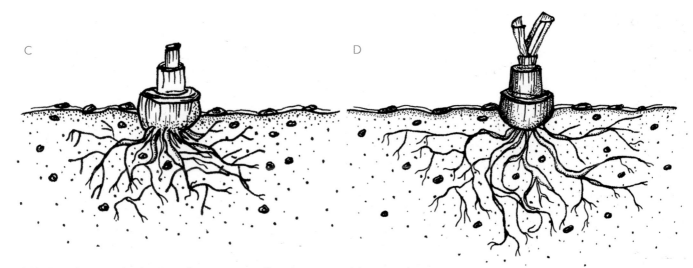

C

Watch as the crown begins to send up a new set of leaves

D

New green leaves appear

CHAPTER THIRTEEN

Maintaining and protecting your garden

A garden is like a child: it needs constant attention if it is to flourish. You will have to do a lot to keep it healthy so that you can harvest good and plentiful crops.

Watering

Vegetables need water to grow well. Young plants must be kept damp. Check the garden every day – in summer, twice a day – to make sure that the soil is not dry. Stick your finger into the top layer of the soil: if it is dry, you need to water.

The best times to water are early in the morning and late in the afternoon. Avoid using a hosepipe because it wastes far too much water. Use a bucket and a watering can made out of a tin (or a plastic bottle) with holes punched in the bottom. Water the area around the plant well.

Unless your plants are very small and their roots are shallow, it is fine if the top few centimetres are dry. Use your finger to check. If you poke deeper than this into the soil and it is still dry, then you need to water.

Here are some ideas for you to conserve water.

Become a "water harvester": catch and store rainwater and dew from your roof…

Catch and store rain water in drums and ponds

Even a small roof can collect a lot of water during light rain.

Many houses do not have gutters but it is easy to fit them. The rain water is then channelled into clean drums, large buckets, old baths or any kind of home-made tank. If you cover the storage container, you will reduce the loss of water through evaporation. To prevent mosquitoes from breeding in the water, add a few drops of cooking oil, which will suffocate them and will not damage your plants.

An improved gutter for catching rainwater

Another idea for catching rain water is to bend a piece of iron sheeting into a "V" shape and place it on wooden poles so that it is supported at a slant. Keep it from blowing away in strong winds by securing it with wire. Catch the water in a drum, which you can place at the lower edge of the bent sheeting.

If your garden is heavily mulched, and you're using a hosepipe to water, there is little point in using a sprinkler, because the water simply does not penetrate through the layers of dry material. It is more effective to stand and water each plant, making sure that the soil around it is soaked. This is called "target watering". You may think that this is an unnecessary waste of time but, in the light of our "holistic" approach to food gardening, you can use the opportunity to relax and unwind, both physically and mentally.

Observe the wildlife in your garden: look and listen. Think about your day, express your gratitude for life unfolding so miraculously around you and breathe in deeply all the fragrances that Nature has produced. In short, this is your meditation time each day.

Try not to get water on the leaves of pumpkins, squash and marrows. Wet leaves encourage the growth of powdery mildew, which stunts the growth of the plants. To avoid wetting the leaves, use a simple system of drip irrigation by burying a plastic bottle next to the spot where you plant the seeds.

> Did you know that only two out of every 100 drops of water actually reach the roots of a plant?
>
> Yes – 98% is wasted through run-off and evaporation by the sun and wind.

Water the roots of plants. Try to avoid wetting the leaves.

*To make sure that irrigation water gets
to the roots of the plants…*

- Make four tiny holes in the lid of a plastic bottle using a hot needle.
- Fill the bottle with water and loosely replace the cap.
- Lay the bottle on the ground at the base of a plant and let the water slowly drip out.
- This is a very simple way of watering the roots of each plant.

If you are watering with a hosepipe, put the end of the pipe right at the base of your plants so that you can be sure that the water gets to where it is needed. Remember that watering the leaves of plants, especially at night, can increase the incidence of plant diseases. Bacteria and fungi love wet leaves.

Practise drip irrigation…

There are several ways of doing this. You can adapt this method easily for your particular garden layout. Make sure that you cover the system with thick mulch to prevent loss of water through evaporation.

A simple method of drip irrigation

A simple bucket-drip system costs very little to set up. All you need is a 16-litre bucket or a plastic drum, either raised off the ground on bricks or supported on a wooden pole about one metre off the ground.

- Attach the fittings to the bottom of the bucket.
- Attach a line of plastic tubing (or old hosepipe).
- Place the bucket close to the vegetable bed to be irrigated.
- Lay the drip tube down the middle of the bed.

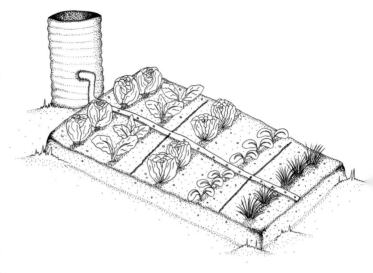

Drip irrigation made simple (and cost-effective)

- With a sharp nail, make holes through the tube at intervals of 20 cm and thread 110 cm lengths of natural-fibre baling twine through each hole.
- Tie a knot in each end of the twine and lay the twine across the length of the bed, running next to each planting line.
- Cover with mulch.
- Plant the vegetables in rows along each dripper line, at the correct spacing for the chosen crop.
- Fill the bucket once in the early morning and, if necessary, in the evening.
- Check with your finger to see whether it is necessary to water.

Weeding

Keep the beds free of weeds because they compete with your vegetable plants for the food and water in the soil. The smaller the weeds are when you pull them out, the less disturbance there will be to the roots of your crops.

Use the weeds to make "weed tea", mulch paths, add to the compost heap or put into the next trench. Diseased weeds must be burnt and the ashes sprinkled in the garden as a fertiliser.

Some weeds, like wild spinach, stinging nettle, chick weed, fat-hen, milk thistle and pigweed, are eaten in relishes and as vegetables. They are highly nutritious. Others are used as medicines. Find out about weeds by asking other gardeners around you.

Mulching

This is one of the most important jobs for any gardener. Soil should never be left exposed to the elements. In Nature, it is always covered either by living plants and their canopies of leaves, or by dead plant and animal remains. So, cover your soil with dry materials, preferably plant waste.

Mulch...

- slowly breaks down or decomposes and feeds the soil with organic matter and improves its structure.
- prevents the garden beds from drying out so you do not have to water so frequently. It keeps water in the soil.
- keeps the soil cool in summer, so that plant roots do not get burnt, and warm in winter.
- slows down or prevents weed growth. You will not have to work so hard!
- encourages earthworms to your garden.
- provides a home for useful creatures – frogs, lizards and snakes – who eat the pests that come to your vegetables.

Mulching is one of those garden practices that you will be doing for ever more. When the wind blows the mulch away, add more. As it decomposes into compost for the soil, add more. You can never afford to stop adding mulch to your garden. If you don't have dry plant waste, cover your soil with newspaper, cardboard and even stones. But, mulch your beds, mulch your paths, mulch everything!

Mulch, mulch, and mulch some more…

Weed control

- Fast-growing crops have an advantage over slow-growing or late-emerging weeds, e.g. mealies, soya beans, sorghum, cow peas.
- Weeds face tough competition when your plants are closer together (you can do this when you have trenched your planting areas). The weeds do not have easy access to sunlight and get smothered.
- Leave the weeds taken out of your beds to form a mulch and to smother any other weeds that germinate.

Shading from the sun

Seedlings, and some of the green leafy vegetables, need protection from very strong sun. Use shade hats or netting sewn from old vegetable bags or cloth.

In some areas, where the temperatures are very high in summer, it is a good idea to shade the garden at the hottest time of the day. Make a shade cover with a frame of rough wood and cover it with dry grass, split reeds or whatever materials you can find.

Wind protection

Wind not only damages your plants but also causes them to wilt, dries out the soil and blows away the mulch and topsoil.

Build wind-breaks next to your beds in order to prevent your plants from being damaged by the wind. You will also prevent too much water from being lost from the soil and your mulch and soil from being blown away.

A hedge of plants of different heights provides an effective wind-break around your vegetable garden or your home. Such a barrier reduces the force of the wind and deflects the wind up and away from the garden. It also provides a habitat for small creatures.

Harvesting

This is also a part of maintaining your garden. As tempting as it may be to leave your splendid cauliflower out in the garden for all the world to see, start picking your vegetables as soon as they are ready. Only pick those that you can use immediately and keep them in a cool, dark place until you are ready to eat them. Freshly picked vegetables are full of goodness and are the most nutritious vegetables to eat. Vegetables left on the plant for too long lose their looks, their taste and nutritional value, and may

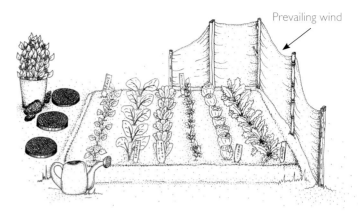

Prevailing wind

A simple, movable windbreak

become fibrous. They are also very likely to be attacked by some pest or other.

Some harvesting tips

- Tomatoes and other fruits should be allowed to ripen on the plant as far as possible. Sun-ripened fruit tastes much better and is full of vitamins. Eat raw for maximum benefit, cooked only by the sun.

- Young vegetables are delicious eaten raw in salads or lightly steamed.

- One or two leaves of lettuce (especially the non-heading varieties) and spinach and a few stalks of celery can be removed from each plant without causing any harm to the plants.

- The more you pick beans and peas, the more the plants will produce.

- Try and grow plants that go on and on producing food for you – such as spinach, beans, peas, tomatoes, Chinese cabbage, New Zealand spinach and peppers. Once you pick a cabbage – that is that!

- Grow plants where you can eat the whole plant. There are lots of examples of these.

- Eat the leaves as well as the roots of carrots. The leaves are delicious chopped into soups and stews and are full of vitamins.
- Beetroot leaves taste better than spinach.
- Turnip leaves are good in soups and stews and are more nutritious than the root.
- Pumpkin leaves, flowers and young shoots are all edible.

You may be able to think of other multiple-use plants. Consult the seed-sowing guides for details of harvesting times for different crops.

Save money: collect your own seed

Seeds are very expensive, so always leave a few of your best plants to go to seed. Tie a piece of red string around the stem so that you will remember not to harvest these plants for eating.

When the seeds are ready (nice and dry), carefully cut off the dry flower heads into a paper bag.

Do not pull them off, as most of the seed will end up being shaken onto the ground. If you cannot find paper bags in the shops, use an old paper packet from sugar or flour, or make one out of newspaper. Just make sure the re-used packets are clean.

Hang the packet in a cool dry place.

Alternatively, hang the flower heads over a baking sheet or a cardboard lid until they have dried out completely and the seeds have dropped off.

Once the dry seeds have all dropped into the bottom of the packet, collect them up and store them in paper envelopes. Never keep them in plastic as they will go mouldy.

Label and date them and store in cool, dry place.

Tie a paper packet around lettuce flowers once they are mature, to catch the seeds

Catch onions seeds in an old stocking tied around the flower head

Some more hints for successful seed saving

One of the problems with saving your own seed is that many crops cross-pollinate. For example, in the squash family, crosses occur between the different types that are flowering at the same time in your, or your neighbour's, garden. This means that, when you come to grow from your seed in the next season, you come up with some weird and wonderful-looking crops that don't look like the plants in the previous season. They'll taste just as good, mind you.

However there are a number of vegetables that self-pollinate – lettuce, tomatoes, peas and beans. So give these a try.

Beans and peas
(including broad beans)
The first pods produced by bean plants are the best for future cultivation. Mark them with a piece of string and let them mature on the plant.

Once the pods are mature, pull up the whole plant and hang it in an airy place, out of the sun. It is better to leave these seeds in the dried pods, storing all the pods in containers before they pop. Watch out for signs of insect attack and discard any affected pods.

Tomato, gooseberry and granadilla seeds
(also baby marrow, cucumbers, pumpkin, butternut and gem squash)
Leave the fruit to fully ripen on the plant. Pick and store on a windowsill until over-ripe (soft and mushy). Cut the fruit open and scoop out the seeds into a container of warm water.

After a few days, the water will go murky and smelly. We say that the mixture is fermenting.

Pour the mixture into a sieve and wash well with clean water to remove all the pulp. Put the cleaned seeds onto a piece of cotton cloth and let them dry before storing.

Another quick and easy method of dealing with small sticky seeds is to smear them onto newspaper or a paper plate. Allow the seeds to dry before folding the paper into an envelope.

Label and date the seed pack, and dry.

You may think that
once your harvest is over, you can sit back.
But no, keep planting.

Replanting

The ideal situation is to pick some fresh food from your garden every single day right through the year. This means that at no time should your vegetable beds have any bare spaces. As soon as a row of vegetables has been harvested, lightly dig over the row, work in some compost and replant the row with another crop.

Remember to rotate your crop so that you are not planting a vegetable from the same family as the one you have just harvested. The way to achieve an even flow of vegetables to the kitchen is to frequently sow small batches every three to four weeks. In this way, you will always have something to eat.

Start a small nursery where you will always have seedlings ready for transplanting into empty rows and beds.

Once you have established your garden and your routine, you will have time to start talking to your neighbours and friends about what you are doing.

Share your ideas and take the time to keep learning new things. You will find that not only have you turned your life into an exciting adventure, but you will start meeting the most interesting people. You will always have something to do and something to learn and share.

But, most important of all, you will always
have something to eat!

Vegetable planting guide for southern Africa

Frost–free areas

Type of vegetable	J	F	M	A	M	J	J	A	S	O	N	D	In rows	Between rows	Planting depth for seeds	Time for seedlings to emerge (days)	Time to harvest (weeks)
Best time to plant (month of year) spans months; **Planting distance (cm)** spans In rows / Between rows																	
ROOT CROPS																	
Beetroot	X	X	X	X		X	X	X	X	X			7–10	20	1cm	10–14	10 (12–15 if cold)
Carrot	X	X	X	X	X	X	X	X	X	X	X	X	5–7	15–20	5mm	10–20	8–14
Leek ++	X	X	X	X	X		X	X	X				15	20	5mm	10–14	16–20
Onion ++			X	X	X		X	X	X				7–10	20	1cm	10–14	24–34
Parsnip			X	X			X	X					15	50	5mm	15–20	16 - 24
Radish	X	X	X	X	X	X	X	X	X	X	X	X	3–5	10–15	5mm	3–5	5–8
Turnip		X	X	X	X		X	X	X	X			10	20	5mm	6–10	10–16
LEAF CROPS AND BRASSICAS																	
Broccoli ++	X	X	X	X	X	X	X	X	X	X			40	50	5mm	6–10	10–16
CM Kale ++	X	X	X	X									30	30	5mm	6–10	8–10
Cabbage ++	X	X	X	X	X	X	X	X	X	X	X		40	50	5mm	6–10	10–16
Cauliflower ++	X	X	X	X	X	X	X	X	X	X	X	X	40	50	5mm	6–10	10–16
Celery ++		X	X										20	30	5mm	14–21	15–20
Chinese Cabbage		X	X	X	X	X							20	30	5mm	6–10	8–12
Lettuce ++	X	X	X	X	X	X	X	X	X	X	X	X	30	30	3–5mm	8–10	10–14
Morogo ++	X							X	X	X			20	25	5mm	7–10	8–12
New Zealand Spinach								X	X	X			50	100	4cm	14–21	10
Parsley ++			X	X	X	X	X	X	X	X	X		20	20	5mm	21	12–14
Rape/Kale ++	X	X	X	X									30	30	5mm	6–10	8–10
Spinach ++		X	X	X	X		X	X	X	X			20	25	1cm	7–10	9–12
FRUIT CROPS																	
Chilli ++							X	X	X	X	X		30	40	5mm	10–14	14–16
Cucumber							X	X	X	X	X		80	25–30	1cm	6–10	16–20
Eggplant ++							X	X	X	X	X		40	50	5mm	10–14	14–16
Kohlrabi	X	X	X	X	X	X	X	X					10–15	25	5mm	6–10	8–10
Marrow (bush types)							X	X	X	X	X		60–80	100	2cm	6–10	12–16
Mealies (green and sweetcorn)							X	X	X	X	X		20	25–35	4cm	7–10	11–12
Pepper ++							X	X	X	X	X		30	40	5mm	10–14	14–16

Type of vegetable	J	F	M	A	M	J	J	A	S	O	N	D	In rows	Between rows	Planting depth for seeds	Time for seedlings to emerge (days)	Time to harvest (weeks)
Pumpkin								X	X	X	X	X	60–80	100	2cm	6–10	14–17
Squash (trailing plants)								X	X	X	X	X	60–80	100	2cm	6–10	10–12
Sweet melon								X	X	X	X	X	60–80	100	2cm	6–10	14–16
Tomato ++							X	X	X	X	X	X	50	75	5mm	10–14	12–20
Watermelon								X	X	X	X	X	60–80	100	2cm	6–10	14–16
LEGUMES																	
Broad beans			X	X	X	X							15–20	50	4 –5cm	10–14	16–18
Bush (dwarf) beans	X	X	X					X	X	X	X	X	10	25	4cm	7–10	10–12
Climbing (runner) beans	X							X	X	X	X		15	25	4–5cm	7–10	10–12
Lucerne			X	X	X		X	X	X				10–15	20	5mm	7–10	8–10
Peas			X	X	X	X	X						20	25	3–4	7–10	14–16
Soya beans								X	X	X			40	50–75	25mm	7–10	18–22
OTHER CROPS																	
Artichoke (globe)	X	X								X	X		100	100	1cm	14	56
Artichoke tubers (Jerusalem)									X	X	X		40	100	12cm	21 –28	20–30
Potato tubers								X	X	X	X	X	30	50	10cm	21–28	16–20
Sunflowers	X						X	X	X	X	X	X	30	100	1cm	5–8	12–20
Sweet potato tubers									X	X	X	X	30–40	50	5cm	28	18–20

Note: X   Best seed planting months
++ Seedlings of these plants can be planted in the same month as the seeds

Areas that experience frost

Type of vegetable	J	F	M	A	M	J	J	A	S	O	N	D	In rows	Between rows	Planting depth for seeds	Time for seedlings to emerge (days)	Time to harvest (weeks)
ROOT CROPS																	
Beetroot	X	X	X	X				X	X	X	X		7–10	20	1cm	10–14	10 (12–15 if cold)
Carrot	X	X	X	X				X	X	X	X	X	5–7	15–20	5mm	10–20	8–14
Leek ++	X	X	X					X	X				15	20	5mm	10–14	16–20
Onion ++			X	X	X			X	X				7–10	20	1cm	10–14	24–34
Parsnip			X	X				X	X				15	50	5mm	15–20	16–24
Radish	X	X	X	X	X			X	X	X	X	X	3–5	10–15	5mm	3–5	5–8
Turnip		X	X	X	X			X	X	X	X	X	10	20	5mm	6–10	10–16
LEAF CROPS AND BRASSICAS																	
Broccoli ++			X	X	X								40	50	5mm	6–10	10–16
CM Kale ++	X	X	X	X									30	30	5mm	6–10	8–10

Type of vegetable	J	F	M	A	M	J	J	A	S	O	N	D	In rows	Between rows	Planting depth for seeds	Time for seedlings to emerge (days)	Time to harvest (weeks)
Cabbage ++		X	X	X	X			X	X	X	X	X	40	50	5mm	6–10	10–16
Cauliflower ++			X	X	X								40	50	5mm	6–10	10–16
Celery ++	X	X	X										20	30	5mm	14–21	15–20
Chinese Cabbage		X	X	X	X								20	30	5mm	6–10	8–12
Lettuce ++			X	X	X			X	X	X			30	30	4mm	8–10	10–14
Morogo ++	X							X	X	X	X		20	25	5mm	7–10	8–12
New Zealand Spinach									X	X	X		50	100	4cm	14–21	10
Parsley ++									X	X			20	20	5mm	21	12–14
Rape/Kale ++		X	X	X	X								30	30	5mm	6–10	8–10
Spinach ++	X	X	X	X	X			X	X	X	X	X	20	25	1cm	7–10	9–12
FRUIT CROPS																	
Chilli ++	X							X	X	X	X		30	40	5mm	10–14	14–16
Cucumber								X	X				80	25–30	1cm	6–10	16–20
Eggplant ++								X	X	X	X	X	40	50	5mm	10–14	14–16
Kohlrabi	X	X	X	X									10–15	25	5mm	6–10	8–10
Marrow (bush types)								X	X	X	X		60–80	100	2cm	6–10	12–16
Mealies (green and sweetcorn)								X	X	X			20	25–35	4cm	7–10	11–12
Pepper ++	X							X	X	X	X		30	40	5mm	10–14	14–16
Pumpkin								X	X	X			60–80	100	2cm	6–10	14–17
Squash (trailing plants)								X	X	X			60–80	100	2cm	6–10	10–12
Sweet melon								X	X	X			60–80	100	2cm	6–10	14–16
Tomato ++								X	X	X	X	X	50	75	5mm	10–14	12–20
Watermelon								X	X	X			60–80	100	2cm	6–10	14–16
LEGUMES																	
Broad beans				X	X	X							20	50	4–5cm	10–14	16–18
Bush (dwarf) beans							X	X	X	X	X		10	25	4cm	7–10	10–12
Climbing (runner) beans								X	X	X			15	25	4–5cm	7–10	10–12
Lucerne			X	X	X	X							10–15	20	5mm	7–10	8–10
Peas			X	X	X								20	25	1cm	7–10	14–16
Soya beans								X	X	X			40	50–75	25mm	7–10	18–22
OTHER CROPS																	
Artichoke (globe)	X	X								X	X		100	100	1cm	14	56
Artichoke (Jerusalem)								X	X	X			40	100	12cm	21–28	20–30
Potato								X	X	X	X		30	50	10cm	21–28	16–20
Sunflowers	X						X	X	X	X	X	X	30	100	1cm	5–8	12–20
Sweet potato tubers								X	X	X			30–40	50	5cm	28	18–20

Note: X Best seed planting months

++ Seedlings of these plants can also be planted in the same month as the seeds

Bibliography/Recommended reading

Altieri, Miguel A. 1998. *Agroecology. The Science of Sustainable Agriculture.* IT Publications

Appelhof, Mary. 1982. *Worms Eat my Garbage: How to Setup and Maintain a Vermicomposting System.* Flowerfield Enterprises

Ball, Jeff. 1988. *Rodale's The Garden Problem Solver: Vegetables, Fruits and Herbs.* Rodale Press

Bailey, David. 2001. Vyvyan Howard in bullet points. *Living Earth* No 211

Bird, Richard. 2003. *Growing Fruit and Vegetables.* London: Hermes House

Buchsbaum, Ralph. 1948. *Animals Without Backbones: 2.* Penguin Books

Carrel, Alex. 1935. *Man, the Unknown.* Harper & Brothers

Carson, Rachel. 1962. *Silent Spring.* Houghton Mifflin

Clarke, James. 1991. *Back to Earth.* Johannesburg: Jacana

Charles Darwin. 1881. *The Formation of Vegetable Mould Through the Action of Earthworms with Observations on their Habits.*

Craig, Sam. 2001. Is organic food really better for you? *Living Earth* No 209

De Villiers, W.M. & Schoeman. 1988. *Garden Pests and Diseases in South Africa.* Cape Town: Struik

Dupriez, Hughes & De Leener, Phillipe. 1989. *African Gardens and Orchards.* London: MacMillan

Elwell, Henry & Maas, Anita. 1995. *Natural Pest and Disease Control.* Zimbabwe: Natural Farming Network

Environmental and Development Agency Trust. 1980. *People's Farming Workbook.* Cape Town: David Philip

Fambidzanai Permaculture Centre. 1998. *Propagating Plants: An Organic Approach.* Harare: Mambo Press

Farmers' Weekly magazine

Filmer, Martin R. 1991. *South African Spiders. An Identification Guide.* Struik

Findhorn Community. 1979. *The Findhorn Garden: Pioneering a New Vision of Man and Nature in Cooperation.* London: Turnstone Books/Wildwood House Ltd

Gerber, Johan. 2006. *The Garden Guardian's Guide to Environmentally-responsible Garden Care.* Cape Town: Aardvark Press

Gilbert, Zoe & Hadfield, Jack. 1992. *Down-to-earth: Fruit and Vegetable Gardening in South Africa.* Cape Town: Struik

Hall, Dudley. 1987. *A Garden of Plenty.* Cape Town: David Philip

Hamilton, Geoff. 1987. *The Organic Garden Book: The Complete Guide to Growing Flowers, Fruit and Vegetables Naturally.* London: DK

Hartmann, Thom. 1998. *The Last Hours of Ancient Sunlight.* New York: Three Rivers Press

Hessayon, D.G. 1985. *The Vegetable Expert.* Waltham Cross: PBI Publications

Hodges, Jeffrey. (Ed.) 1995. *The Natural Gardener: A Complete Guide to Organic Gardening.* New South Wales: Angus & Robertson

Howard, Sir Albert. 1940. *An Agricultural Testament.* Oxford University Press

Illustrated Encyclopaedia of Gardening in South Africa. 1984. Reader's Digest Association

Joubert, Leonie S. 2006. *Scorched. South Africa's Changing Climate.* Wits University Press

Kenton, Susannah & Kenton, Leslie. 1994. *Raw Energy.* London: Vermilion

Kenton, Branton. 1987. *Quantum Carrot.* London: Ebury Press

King, Alan N. 1985. *Agriculture: An Introduction for Southern Africa.* Cambridge: Cambridge University Press

Knight, Carol. 2004. *Miracles of Hope.* White Rock Publishers

Lovelock, James. 2006. *The Revenge of Gaia.* Allen Lane

McGrath, Mike. (Ed.) 1996. *The Best of Organic Gardening.* Rodale Press

Mollison, B. & Slay, Reny Mia. 1991. *Introduction to Permaculture.* Zimbabwe: Tutorial Press, and Australia: Tagari Publications

Mollison, B. 1988. *Permaculture: A Designers' Manual.* Tagau Publications

Murphy, David. 2005. *Organic Growing with Worms. A Handbook for a Better Environment.* Australia: Viking

Myers, Norman. (Ed.) 1985. *The Gaia Atlas of Planet Management* . London: Pan Books

Nancarrow, Loren & Hogan Taylor, Janet. 1998. *The Worm Book.* California: Ten Speed Press

Nancarrow, Loren & Hogan Taylor, Janet. 2000. *Dead Daisies Make Me Crazy.* California: Ten Speed Press

Nancarrow, Loren & Hogan Taylor, Janet. 2000. *Dead Snails Leave No Trails.* California: Ten Speed Press

Palmer, Eve & Pitman, Norah. 1972. *Trees of Southern Africa. Volumes 1, 2 and 3.* A.A. Balkema: Cape Town

Picker Mike, Griffiths, Charles, Weaving, Alan. 2002. *Field Guide to Insects of South*

Pimentel, David. 1973. Extent of pesticide use, food supply and pollution. *Proc. N.Y. Ent. Soc.* 81:13–33

Richard, David & Byers, Dorie. (Ed.) 1998. *Taste Life! The Organic Choice.* Vital Health Publishing

Rollin Spencer, Edwin & Bergdolt, Emma. 1974. *All About Weeds.* Courier Dorer

Rosenberg, Alan & Linders, Thomas. 2006. *Global Health in Crisis: The Answer Lies in the Soil.* South Africa: Lindros

Roux, Marie. (Alias Nokwenza). 1978. *Grow to Live: A Simple Guide to Organic Cultivation and Self-sufficiency.* Self-published

Ryrie, Charlie. 2001. *Compost.* London: Gaia Books Ltd

Thompson, Ken. 2008. *An Ear to the Ground. Understanding Your Garden.* Transworld

Thorsons, Grian. 1996. *The Gardener.* Harper Collins

Tompkins, Peter & Bird, Christopher. 1998. *The Secret life of Plants.* Alaska: Earthpulse Press Incorporated

Seymour, John. 1981. *The Complete Book of Self-sufficiency.* London: Corgi Books

Smith, Barry. 2006. *The Farming Handbook.* Interpak Books

Steiner, Rudolf. n.d. *Agriculture.* New York: Anthroposophic Press

Stout, Ruth & Clemence, Richard. 1979. *The Ruth Stout No-work Garden Book.* Rodale Press

Van Wyk, Ben-Erik & Gericke, Nigel. 2000. *People's Plants. A Guide to Useful Plants of Southern Africa.* Pretoria: Briza Publications

Vukasin, Helen L., Roos, Loes, Spicer, Newton & Davies, Mike. 1995. *Production Without Destruction.* Zimbabwe: Natural Farming Network

Young, Robert & Redford, Shelley. 2002. *The pH Miracle.* Time Warner.

Your Gardening Questions Answered: A Practical Guide for the South African Gardener. 1989. Reader's Digest Association